DO IT ANYWAY: THE SINGLE MOM'S GUIDE TO

LIVING LIFE AND ACHIEVING HER GOALS

by

Kaywanda Lamb

Do It Anyway!
The Single Mom's Guide To Living Life and Achieving Her Goals

ISBN-13: 978-1503120891
ISBN-10: 1503120899

Printed in the United States of America.

Note: This book is intended to inform the reader and to be a guide based on the life, research, and experiences of the author. It is not legal advice. Readers are advised to consult a professional counselor, coach, or other qualified professional. The reader assumes all liability for actions they take based on information in this book. Every attempt has been made to ensure the accuracy of the information provided, but the author assumes no liability or responsibility for any errors that may exist. The facts and theories on parenting, love, and relationships with children and adults are subject to interpretation of the reader, and the conclusions presented by the author may not agree with other interpretations.

Dedication:

This book is dedicated to my sons, Syon and Kamron. My love for them and my desire to provide a better way of life for them have been the catalysts and the catapults that have pushed me for the last fifteen years. I personally have grown because of my fierce love for them and their ability to have a good life. They are the two people I fuss at the most only because I want them to be great, only because I see how great they are … only because they are my heart.

Because you had needs, I was determined to make a way. It was for you to have a better life that I worked as hard as I did and still do today. May you learn what hard work and true love are from me. Let no one tell you what you cannot do. Instead, show them how to *Do It Anyway!*

I also dedicate this book to the sweet spirit and memory of my nephew Chris Wright who died too young. May his love for life and his genuine curiosity dwell in us all. See you one day in the sweet by-and-by!

Table of Contents

Acknowledgments
Introduction

Acknowledgments

This journey has not been easy, and for that I am thankful. It is the gut-wrenching issues of life that make us who we really are. I want to acknowledge the men and women who see greatness in me and remind me daily to chase the purpose God has given me.

My best friend, Stephanie Roach, is the first entrepreneur I've seen go from nothing to something. As a college student, she and her then boyfriend, Lamount Roach, had a dream to "have" something—and they did it, numerous times over. They were my first examples of bravery, hard work, true friendship, and never-give-up attitude. I salute you both for always having my back.

To my Aunt Johnnie, I say thank you for making sure I never regretted going to college in your city. (Smile.) Thank you for always having a listening ear late in the midnight hour and for showing me that a woman can raise a man. You did it! I know I can!

The next person I want to thank is resting in heaven, but she is the reason I am who I am. Therestha Lamb is the grandmother every child needs—the kind who inspires you to Do It Anyway! She cheered me on every step of the way, and when I fell, she said, "Get back up." I owe her a debt of gratitude the ocean cannot fill.

To my tribe, you know who you are. Too numerous to name, but you are the wind beneath my wings. Thank you, sisters and brothers on the journey, for your love and support. Together, we all win, as Michelle Y. Talbert says. I am grateful for you.

Introduction:

"The ratio of men to women is 4 to 1."
"Single women may never marry."
"If you have kids, your odds are ... blah, blah, blah."

The statistics start out something like that, right? Well, aren't
you tired of hearing it all? I know I am. So how about you take
yourself out of those scenarios? How about you *create* the life
you want, whether Boaz comes or not?

This book is designed to teach you to look within and *find your
own power, fire, and truth*. This book will give you the tools to live
them out—fiercely!

You'll make it *nowhere* listening to what *they* have to say. But if
you turn off the latest report on life, love, parenting, work, etc.
and focus in on you, you'll see that *you can do this thing*!

So, you're a single parent. My guess is that, like me, you didn't
plan to be. So now what? It's earth shattering—I agree ... until
you learn to live and love again.

Are you going to just raise your babies alone, have a ho-hum
life, and handle the usual day-to-day parenting, *OR* are you
going to live an exciting life that includes you raising your babies
AND living your dreams?

A popular psychiatrist says that after divorce, a parent should
focus on the kids and not date. Listen, I'm all for focusing on
the kids, but the part about "not having anyone" to do life with
is *NOT OKAY* with me. I mean, what planet is she on?

In *Do It Anyway!*, we're going to discuss how you can do both *well.*

Are you ready to dig in and do the work? Are you ready to have YOUR best life now? Then, let's get to it. I have outlined twelve lessons I followed to get from gloomy to happy. Notice I said that I *learned*. I don't want you to have to go as long as I did to get out of the "woe is me" mindset. I want you to live! Your kids deserve the best you. Give her to them *now*!

If this is a challenge you're ready to face, turn the page. Let's do this!

STEP 1: HEAL

I sat across from one of my best friends on a sunny Saturday afternoon in my apartment listening attentively as she spoke. We were having *the usual* girl talk while our kids played video games. We had figured out that our "girl time" was when our kids were enjoying each other. Yassss! Fun times!

This time, though, was a little off. She was whining. Again. So it wasn't much fun. The conversation was typical. Nothing new. This was our much needed "mommy break," yet we were spending it on *old* news. It went something like this: "I don't know why he doesn't help me with the kids. Every time I ask for help, he gives me an excuse," she angrily said for the millionth time, her eyes rolling to the back of her head.

All I could think was, *Are we really having this same discussion? Again!* Now, don't get me wrong. I had those moments too. I admit it. I was once like that: *Angry. Bitter. Frustrated. Too through!*

A very long time ago, I was disappointed in my kids' dad, in myself, and in my choices. I was tired of the lies—just like my friend. Over time, though, I learned that it's pointless to complain about a person who, for whatever reason, is not fulfilling their parental responsibility. I learned to let *it*, and *them*, go. My girlfriend eventually had to learn to do the same thing. Her children deserved better. She deserved better. Her new, wonderful man that she would eventually meet deserved better. But she would never have any of that unless she healed from the hurt. Get the picture?

Healing is a part of the journey to have what you truly want.

You might say, "Well, how was she broken?" or "How were you in need of healing?" The answer is simple. When you love someone and they hurt you, you find yourself on a roller-coaster ride feeling happy, sad, misused, abused, etc. The emotions swell up in you, and you lose your mind. It breaks you to love them. You are confused and lonely because you're in a relationship but not really. Then, you find yourself in love on and off. There is mistrust and you keep trying to . Compound this with children, and now it's a soap opera that just got real. If you aren't careful, you'll think that's love. My girlfriend was showing signs of something I had already seen and gone through. Coping and soothing a broken heart that kept healing and re-breaking because she (and I) were trying to love someone who didn't know how to love us in the first place. That's not love, but if we are not careful, we'll think it is.

When you love someone, you endure a lot. If you're not careful, you'll look up and will have spent years trying to get a broken person to love you back. Breaking free from that boyfriend was the best thing she ever did. Breaking free from my ex was the best thing I've ever done. You, sweet sister, have to do the same.

So we all have to detox from these wrong messages about love.

The messages we hear that say love is supposed to be this up-and-down roller-coaster ride and that one day it will all work out because we fought for our love are ALL lies. Don't waste your life looking for potential. It won't work. When it ends, you'll have to walk away from it and *all* the drama. Now, I'm not saying that things don't sometimes work out, but I don't want you waiting around on potential. If and when that wrong relationship bursts, you will have to do the emotional work to get to the point where you feel you're yourself again. And you know what? That takes time, but love *is* worth it. If this is where you are right now, please know you will love again, and you will smile again. I promise. But, if you can save yourself some heartache, do it. Look at what you see now not at what you hope or want to see. Move on and heal.

I want you to be alive and loving your life. You should thrive in your relationships. When you truly are alive and enjoying life, you will know it because you will be at peace. That is what I mean by healing. When there is peace in your life and heart, you behave differently, you see life differently, and you exude the fact that you are healed. The heart is a beautiful thing, but when it's hurt, it shows in your words, in your actions, and in your facial expressions. Bad relationships bring out the bad in us. They break us for a season, but they cannot (if we decide to move on) break us forever. Let go and heal.

There is no hiding a broken soul. You must heal it.

People withdraw, become distrustful and are downright bitter when they're going through the healing process. I know because I was there. My friend was there. You may even be there, too. When a relationship dissolves and we didn't expect or want it to the evil twin comes out. She annoys everyone in her path and makes our real lives a hot mess. Our bad attitude because we're hurting is amplified more than it should be. We behave opposite of the sweet amazing women we are. For a season. Thank God, it's only for a season!

Sis, this kind of behavior does not describe Ruth (Biblical character who got her man after going through loss, pain, and struggle). And if you're looking for a Boaz, he's not looking for the qualities I've listed in a woman. You want a *whole* man. Right? Well, he wants a *whole* woman. Healing is necessary to be able to know, accept, and be real love. Just wait—I go into detail about Ruth and Boaz in chapter 9. So hold on and go through the healing process of being bitter, hating his guts, whining about it all, and getting over it. As dramatic as that all sounds, don't short-circuit your process. It may take you less time than you think and you will be so glad you allowed all those feelings to run their course. It's best to do this now instead of in the relationship with your dream guy who is not expecting you to have unresolved issues.

I know it may be painful to admit that you need help, but let me tell you—it's exactly what you need. Listen, are you still going around the same mountain of back and forth love, negative self-talk or griping about the ex, or even maintaining a "woe is me" single mindset? It's okay if you are. I just want you to know that talking about it will not change him. Worrying and thinking about it will not change him. Being down on yourself will not change the situation. What you must do is heal. Keep reading to find out why you must and how you can do it and move on to your best life.

Through many tears, prayers, laughs, and conversations like the one we had above, my friend realized she was better off without her ex and so were her kids. It's awful, isn't it, that a person could walk away from some beautiful babies who did nothing to them? But it happens every day.

Maybe you decided to have a baby without having the father in your and your child's lives? Maybe you're divorced and it was so unexpected that you're still reeling from it? I'm not sure. But what you, my girlfriend, and I have in common is that we are single parents. We are in this role and our kids are counting on us to make things happen, to provide, and to love them the way they deserve. And, you know you what? You can do all of this AND love again.

We do this remarkable work of loving little people, providing for them, and showing them the best life we can. Unfortunately, we do it alone. That connects us, sis, gives us common ground, and creates community. And until we change our status by dating and marrying a good man worthy of us (and our kids), we are *single moms*. However, *single* doesn't mean bitter, broken, destitute, or incapable of moving on, so don't let your status define you. You are a mom! You are giving your babies what they need. So what you do it alone! You are showing up and owning your "awesome" by telling life "I will not die here. I will *live* and *love* again. My babies are blessed because I am taking care of us."

Defy your status by rocking the life you got!

Speaking of being connected, I sincerely hope you and every single mom you know have learned to connect, encourage, and inspire another sister whether she's white, black, brown, or blue. Rich or poor, we all need a village. No one in their right mind asks or even wants to parent alone. (I said *right* mind.) When it happens, though, we must not spend time on why we are alone. Instead, we must mobilize and live on. After all, we have babies to take care of, and they deserve only the best. It's not easy to do, but do it you must. You must take care of them AND yourself. So, connect with other single moms, use your resources, and resolve to do it anyway! Resolve to live and thrive anyway!

In order to get to the good part—and trust me, there is a good part—you've got to go through this stage of dealing with the pain, letting go of what went wrong, and healing. Don't pass it up, pretending to be Superwoman. You're human. It's okay. Just don't stay there longer than needed. Remember, your best life is ahead of you and not behind.

Let Go

Letting go of someone who isn't there for you and your kids is the best thing you can do for yourself, but it's not easy. I know. I've been there, and I've done that. Regardless, it's the best move you can make, and it will ultimately make your life so much easier. Your objective is to live at peace, in love, and in good health so that you can be around to see your children grow. You must devote your energy to doing the best you possibly can for yourself and your children. No one should be able to cause you to have less than God's best for your life, even if that someone is you. You must let go of everything and everyone that would keep you from having God's best.

In this book, I want to talk about twelve steps you need to take to move you in the right direction for your life. I went through them all. My whole story is so rugged and raggedy that I can't tell it all in this book. So, if you think what you've been through is too hard to get over, think again. But, I've picked certain parts to show you that if I can do it, you can do it. Take every step and apply it to your life. You are coming up out of this!

Sis, if your past is still open, you cannot smoothly move in the present and reach for your future as you feel life calling you to be more. If you are reliving what someone else did, or if you keep bringing it up in every conversation you have, you will not progress because you're reminding yourself of the negative moments, comments, experiences you've had. That is back in the past. LET IT GO!
If you're whining and pining for the past, you cannot see the gifts the present has for you. And trust me, your present has many gifts for you. But, your focus can't be fixed on the wrong thing. You have to have your eyes open to see the beauty of your right now. You can't be asleep coasting through your life, barely making it because your heart is hurting.

If you're not awake in your present, your future is certainly delayed.

It will take you longer to have the best God has for you because you won't let go of the less *you think is the best* and heal. So I beg you, sister, (for your present and for your future, which is *limitless*) let it go.

How do you let go?

I can hear you say, "But I love him!" Yes, you do. But does he love you? Is he there, showing you his love and providing for you and your family? Does he show signs of maturity and progress, of wanting to return to do his part, or of even marrying you? You've got to ask those questions. No living in the memories of the past here. Just focus on the facts. Ask yourself the hard questions and believe what reality is showing you. The person you still love may not be *who he actually is*. I was there. Oh, I was there right in this very spot of loving a man who seemingly loved me, but after our romantic demonstration of love there was no outward demonstration. AT ALL. Let me tell you that a strong physical connection can trick us into thinking that emotional and mental connection is strong. That is why after going through my years of healing, I decided to become celibate. Celibacy helps me date with clarity and stick to my standards. It may not be for you, but I encourage

14

you to refrain from the physical so you can clearly see what you actually have in a man.

Think on that. Soul ties, those physical connections to people that keep you bound to them, are real and usually come from romantic relationships gone sour. One party is left still loving the other because the physical ties connect them are so strong, yet the other person has moved on because they no longer desire the connection. Usually, men are the ones who can move on because society has trained them to love a woman's body and not her mind. Honey, they can tell you what you want to hear, even have kids with you, and walk away with no remorse. For whatever reason, this is just the truth. So, if you do not want to have a "soul tie" to a man who can do that to you, you have to heal, learn from the experience, and make a plan for your life that includes how you will date from here on out.

I definitely had a soul tie to my kid's dad. He wasn't my type and I'll go into that a bit more later. But, that physical draw and the "not having a plan" for what I wanted in a man led me down a path I didn't wanna go down. I know the strong pull to be with a person, to want to marry them, to serve them, and to be with them forever based SOLEY on the physical. Now, ain't that crazy? He did nothing to help financially hardly with the kids, didn't honor me and introduce me as the love of his life, shower me with gifts, be a gentleman and show me what I meant to him, etc. I had no sense because I was physically tied to him.

See, the body lies and the mind believes.

So, when you find yourself in a relationship, and even if you are still in one now, pay attention to who the person is and not on just what they *say*. I share this to help you move on and heal. This is why I don't share my body with men I date. I want to see who they really are before I progress any further. What is his character? Who is he really? Does he honor women? Does he have a healthy self-esteem? If he is a father, does he take care of his children?

Watch the fruit sis before you taste it!

Yes, single parenting will teach you some sense. Lol! I have learned, and I want to help you. Again, the way to cure all this is to focus on reality. What are their actions showing you? Not their words—their actions. Also, how are you all fit spiritually? I guarantee you're not the same. You have to do some praying to remove unhealthy relationships from your life. If it's too much for you, get some help. Soul ties are real, but they can be broken.

Look closely to see if there is actually a relationship. It could be comfort masquerading as relationship because you can relive the good times with a person so much that you forget how they actually are now, in the present. Been there. Listen, wanting the past to return will keep you stuck. Who are they NOW? Forget comfort and the notion that you would have to learn a new person so it's best to keep what you have. All lies! This is your life! Live it happy, healthy, whole, and healed!

Release what no longer serves you!

Still, letting go isn't easy. I admit it. It's especially difficult if you loved hard and if you complicated the matter by having a child. Don't get me wrong: I'm not saying it's easier to get over a heartache without kids. I'm just saying it's different. It's a hard thing to heal while you're expected to keep living as if the heartache didn't happen. Unfortunately, my sweet sister, *that* you must do. "How do you do it?" you say. There's no easy fix, but first, you must decide to move on. Moving forward offers you many opportunities.

As you have seen, I've been in a messy place and am now in a blessed place. I'm so happy to be where I am because I know what it's like to have no mental peace, a broken heart, and feeling for a fool. I know you may be able to relate to some of this, so how did I do it? Let me tell you what got me going in my healing process and on to letting go. My boys were two years old and two months old when I realized their dad and I were not going to work things out. I saw that this person and I could not and would not be able to function as a family unit. It was hard to swallow. *I hadn't planned on dating him—let alone having two kids—and you mean to tell me I'm a single momma!* was all I was thinking when I got pregnant. This is why I say you must have a plan for your life and sis, you must guard it.

You'll end up places you don't want to be, being nice to folks you never should have spoken to—but that's another book.

So, as I was thinking, *This can't be my life*, I had to prepare for my first child. It wasn't supposed to be like this. I was supposed to be ready, married, in love, and living in a nice home with my dreams chased and living the life I saw on

TV! When the babies came and we fell apart, all I could do was look at those beautiful, unsuspecting faces and resolve to *Do It Anyway*. Yes, it sucked. Yes, it wasn't right. But I knew I had to make sure they had food, shelter, clothing, safety, and—most importantly—love. I knew I needed to make sure they had it whether he helped out or not. I had the weight of making sure the day to day went fine when he only popped in every now and again for physical comfort to pacify me, and to be a good dad for a day, and I'm sure to make himself think he was doing his part. It wasn't enough. But, I made it and you will, too.

Unbearable Pain and Open Doors

Let me give some backstory. The first years of my boys' lives, I tried to make things work with a man I hadn't planned on doing anything with but holding a conversation. Really. That's all I had intentions to do. But, I ended up losing my virginity and having not one but two kids with a man I barely knew. In trying to keep together a badly built relationship where I had fallen for the dude, I lost a whole lot of me in the process. If you can relate, please know you can heal. You can move on, and you can love again.

In those years, I took what I shouldn't have, listened to everyone's advice except my own, and really tried to have the American dream made from an *American mess*. There was no fixing this. There was too much for me to forgive and accept. (Have you been there? Can you relate?)

After it was over, their dad and I went on to have years of ugly exchanges via phone and email. He eventually stopped helping, and I became a full-fledged single momma. When my oldest was six, a wonderful thing happened. I changed careers, and an opportunity came up for me to move to a different state. Whether you are a person of faith or not, you have to believe that the way this story is about to turn is nothing but the hand of God at work in my life.

As I was saying, I was a full-fledged single mom and had changed careers when an opportunity arose. I was in disbelief that my life could change so quickly for the better once I made a move in the right direction. It was exciting. I prayed to see if I needed to go on the interview because I was so scared of being in a different place but excited nonetheless. I went to the interview and was offered the job. *Yaasss!* I then prayed to see if I should take the job. I had no sleep the entire weekend. I felt God telling me to go. I heard the little nudges you get in your spirit that say "This is for you. It's your time. Go." I had no family in the new city, but I would have cousins an hour away if I took the job. It was clear. It was time to heal. At the end of the weekend, I knew God was telling me to move. (Now, this isn't to say you need to move, but moving was the best thing I've ever done.)

Because I heeded the call to move, I had three years of peace and absolute bliss in my new city: the ex could no longer promise to come get them anymore and fail to show up (he still did, but not as much), I didn't have to deal with the women he slept around with pretending to be my friends at work and outside the office, and I had the opportunity to start anew. The two of us not being together was the best thing I could have done for me. Raising my boys alone was a blessing in the absence of emotional and mental abuse, infidelity, lying, lack of emotional and financial support, etc. I was able to live again! I was able to make new friends, learn new places, explore and experience NEW everything.

A fresh start will do you good.

Let me say something here: As women, we put up with a lot from men that we should just walk away from in the beginning before our feelings grow deeper. We call it love when it's abuse, indifference, incompatibility, lust, etc. I thank God often for moving me physically so that he could heal me emotionally of that whole experience with my kids' dad. And as you can see, it was hell on wheels. Women everywhere were saying he was sleeping with them. I had small kids to parent and I had to work. It was draining trying to sort through it all to find the truth. I felt dumb and betrayed after it all went down, and moving away helped me to focus and heal. If you are in that space, go through it. Allow yourself to accept your part in it, but reject the feeling to wallow and pout. Your process has an expiration date. After I moved, my life changed. It was my time to heal. Let me show you how I did it.

As a side note, I mentioned the infidelity and messiness with women so that you can see why I was elated to move and ready for a change. All of this was happening in a small college city. My heart ached. I didn't understand why this was happening to me. I was hurting, and I knew I had to heal. I had to make a clean break. *You must as well.*

If you're dealing with a man like that, know that you're not alone. Do what's best for you and your kids. Trust me honey, you can do so much better!

The move was also good for me because before I moved, I was constantly tired. Doing it all, raising the kids, working a full-time job, going to school, etc. made me an exhausted mama. Have you been there? If so, just know it's normal, and try to see what you can cut out of your schedule in order to get more rest. You just keep on providing for you and your babies. It's worth it. Exhausted, with tears in your eyes honey, keep providing.

I remember that as I was going through (healing and dealing), my family and friends were so helpful. They supported me, watch the boys, and were that emotional support I needed. I'm so thankful for them, but the emotional toil of it all was so strong it was keeping me up at night. *Is she my friend? Did he sleep with her, too?* I would wonder. Loving a man like that is sheer foolishness. I've ben there, and I'm telling you that a man who will play games with your heart, your body, your love is a FOOL and unfit for someone as awesome as you! Girl, let it go! Listen, the disrespect I saw and heard—chile! I will write about it when I feel like bringing that up again and if I sense it will help someone else. Other than that—*I MOVED ON! And* so should you!

What my move taught me about releasing the past and living again

Don't discount the benefits of doing something for yourself. A change of scenery will do you good. Simply being in a new space brought on excitement, rejuvenation, adventure, and happiness for me. I was able to lie down at night and sleep. I know some women who would love a good night's sleep trying to hold on to a man who stays out until the wee hours of the morn believing he is with his homies. Listen, I slept so good no longer plagued by his absence in his kid's lives while he while very much present in the same city we lived in. I was in my new place- my blessed place. My kids were safe. We were happy. I had three years of bliss I hadn't had before. Listen, life took a turn for me when I met my boy's dad. I ended up somewhere I hadn't planned on, experiencing emotions and heart hurt I didn't know possible, but God gave me peace when he opened up a new door I also had not seen. My word to you is "Open your eyes. Where are your new doors?"

Now when he called, I wasn't disappointed. When he never made good on his promises I wasn't upset because I couldn't say he was just fifteen minutes away and could get his boys on the weekend. Now he was four and a half hours away. (Of course, people drive farther than that for items incomparable to their kids, but we won't go there cause again we're dealing with a fool and not a man that wants to be a father.) In the early years (because even though we were not together, I wanted my boys to continue to have some interaction with their dad. I foolishly believed that their dad wanted the same). So, I offered to meet him halfway and to bring them during summers. No takers. As usual. But I was OVER IT because I had found my life. So sis, get on with living your life with someone who wants to treat you and your children well.

Starting out in my new city, like I said, was scary. I'm not going to tell you I was fearless. But I did it anyway! Guess what?

It changed my life.

As any young single mom would be, I was excited to start over, yet I was cautious. The boys were young, so I didn't feel I had negatively impacted them by the move. You know our decisions affect our kids so we must always consider them when making decisions. But, in this instance, at this time, the person who needed order, peace, and a plan was *me*. I knew I had to let it all go. I had to release him. *I had to heal.* Here's what I did to get over my ex and on to living my best life in my new city:

1. I made prayer a constant.
2. I did the hard work of forgiving myself.
3. *I did the hard work of forgiving him.*
4. I focused on my boys.
5. I made new friends and tried new things.
6. I spent time alone figuring out what I wanted.
7. I started new endeavors—even with fear present, and shaking in my boots, I started.
8. I stayed focused on my faith.
9. Even when I felt sorry for myself, I dealt with the lies and did not allow them to stop me.
10. I nurtured my family so that we could be strong together.

Notice, I didn't make a plan and decide to get over him. I made conscious steps to get and *do* better. That's all you have to do to get moving—make a decision. None of us can see the future entirely. We don't know how long it will take us to get clarity. But, we can see the present. And if your present isn't what you want, be courageous enough to change it.

No matter what, forgive!

I don't care what it was or who it was that hurt you. You've got to move past it. I had to unlearn some things that life had taught me, and you will, too. Just because you went through it doesn't mean it's the final truth. Just because it happened doesn't mean this is it for you. Reteach yourself the good you want to see in your relationships. It's hard. You may need to get help to do it. But by all means, do it. Release the past so that you can enjoy your present and your glorious future.

Release *you*!

You thought this was all about the other person? The bad one, the one who didn't stay? The one you loved and they STILL left, died, or divorced you? Nope. It's also about you letting go of the hurt you continue to inflict on yourself. I've been there. I know you're doing it, too. See, no one party has all the blame. You can beat yourself up about what you should have done, said, or been, but in the end when it's all over, you're a single parent. You have to deal with this. It sucks. I get it. But for yourself, your sanity, and your kid's sake—let it go. Release you of the hurt, the pain, the what ifs. Release!

This song of "I should have…" will replay in your head and out in your life until you release it. Let God have it. HE does a great job with our messes. Being upset with where you are will not change *where* you are. Only you can make it better from here on out by releasing yourself and by releasing him. Read on to find out "how on Earth" you are to forgive a man that hurt you.

Forgive.

This is the hard part when you're hurting. I know the feeling, the anger, the resentment, the "But you don't know what I've been through" response to anything and anyone trying to get you to come to your senses. I know it all. But sis, you've got to forgive him, and you've got to forgive yourself. No matter who hurt you whether it was the ex, or in my case the ex and his women, you forgive them. If they don't want to see you to hear your apology, *you do the work and walk on into your new life.* To truly be able to *Do It Anyway*, you've got to heal, and forgiving is part of healing. Do it now! It's for your benefit. Now, I'm not saying forgive so that it only benefits you. I'm saying forgive for yourself and for them.

This is something I know well. I've seen it. I had to do it. It wasn't easy. I did it and picked it up again. On and on it went until my journey to healing was over and I was healed. It may be easier for you, or it may be harder. For you and your family, do it anyway! Do it mad, glad, indifferent, sad, etc. DO IT!

Forgiveness sets you free to live the life you deserve.

Years removed from being with my kids' dad, I still had not forgiven him. I was in my new city and enjoying my new life. I mean I was absolutely thrilled about my new job, new digs, new friends, and new experiences. Me and my boys were thriving and life was good. Except I thought I had forgiven him, but I hadn't. How did I *know?* The mention of his name still made me frown, turn up my nose, and bite my tongue to avoid saying something ugly about him in the presence of my kids. It was small, but I still had ugly feelings toward him. Do you know small things can cause big problems? I never got my closure. I never got the why he chose me to have kids with and not respect or honor me. I was harboring unforgiveness because I was waiting on my phone call that said "I'm sorry."

One Sunday I was at a church service, and the pastor said something so poignant it pricked my spirit. He said, "Even if the person is not physically present, alive, or even wants to see you, you forgive them." *What?* I thought. *That can be done?* That clicked so hard for me because I was living a better life, but *it wasn't my best life.* Not yet.

True, I was no longer complaining about him. In fact, I thought I was over him, but the hurt still lingered from time to time. Every time I looked at my beautiful boys, I saw him. God took me through a healing process when I changed states. No one knew about the pain I'd gone through. I was happy and doing it. But deep down, I had not forgiven him or myself. Praise God I was in that church service. I prayed, and I let go. I also asked myself for forgiveness, and I forgave their dad and all the women who had been my fake friends. My life *began* that day, and I haven't looked back. Are you ready to begin living? Then let it go. Forgive him, them, or whoever and LIVE!

You cannot have your best life being bitter, stuck, and resentful.

It doesn't work that way. Like the Esurance commercial where the grandma is showing her friend her Facebook wall. You know the one where she's using actual Polaroids so her friend says "That's not how this works"? Like her friend, you cannot harbor unforgivingness and draw goodness to you. It doesn't work like that. You must release the negativity to attract the positivity you seek. Now, I'm not saying you don't have a nice life. I'm saying you're not experiencing all you can because you're bound by your unwillingness to forgive, which breeds anger, jealousy, discontent, crankiness, separation of relationships, and more!

The rest of your life is waiting on you to get past the hurt.

Yes, it's hard raising children and having to heal at the same time. Betrayal, infidelity, divorce, death—they all hurt, but live on you must. Isn't it time you got to the business of what you were made to do? Isn't it time you got ready for the good part of your life?

You'll have what you want when you heal.

Now, some bitter folks have been successful, so I'm not saying it's impossible. *Smile.* I'm saying that for you to have your best life, you've got to be okay with that part of your life being OVER. Don't carry the hurt any longer. Pray for them and then release them. Pray for yourself and the path for you and your kids to take. You must be healed in order to walk into your future. It's waiting on you. Go get it!

Action Steps: How to Get to Your Healed Place

1. Release him, them, or whatever is holding you back.
2. Do the work, the work of *letting go*. Please go through whatever you must to get to the place of peace you desire.
3. Pray a lot. My faith has been a huge factor in moving on and up. I encourage you to find your faith!
4. Try again to release and live free when you get mad, and remember the pain or when you want to have a pity party.
5. Repeat steps 1–4 as needed.
6. Understand this is a process. It won't be over until you're ready to finally let go. The good news is you *can heal and move on.*

Now, take a moment and journal the steps you're going to take to move toward your future. There is power in writing down your goals. God bless you sis! You're coming out of this!

Write below what you're going to do to make sure you heal. Think of a time frame that you alone know. Plot your course and list what you can do now to get moving in your destiny.

_____

_____

_____

_____

_____

_____

_____

_____

_____

_____

_____

_____

_____

_____

_____

_____

_____

_____

_____

_____

_____

_____

_____

When you change, your life changes

STEP 2: FIND YOUR WHY

It's amazing to see women *who undervalue* what it is they do. I'm always amazed at my girlfriends who tell me they don't have a talent. As women, we singlehandedly make the world go round for our families, yet they—these strong women—think they don't have what it takes to be more, to do greater acts than the mundane, to be great in their own right. They *think* they're regular. In their own words, they're talentless. What they really mean is they don't fully *own* all that they possess, and for some reason they don't know what it is that makes them truly feel alive and *live*. And when I say *live*, I mean that "thing" that pushes their soul to sheer and complete happiness. That "thing" that drives them to wake up and chase their dreams, that *je ne sais quoi* that only they possess. They simply don't know what it is. Or they don't have the courage to admit it.

The Heavy Truth

I think that these women—and you may be one—have lost their "it," their "thing," their "mojo" that God innately placed in them. There's nothing wrong with devoting yourself to your family. In fact, it's quite common for new moms to let go of who they are to become a "we." It's exciting to be married or in a relationship, and to have a new baby is exhilarating. And we go all-in. And of course as single moms, we throw ourselves into the work of being mommy AND daddy because we *think* we have to do so. We, too, go all-in.

This is the part where we all mess up (yes, I also did this). The problem is we begin to neglect ourselves for the benefit of US. When you stay lodged in "we," you begin to lose "I." Make no mistake about it. There is an "I" in fam-i-ly. I know you have good intentions. So did I. But there will come a time when you're going to want to pick up those dreams of being a doctor, of saving the children of the world, of helping the elderly, and a cute, cuddly baby with a wonderful "boo thang" to boot simply will no longer suffice. Hear me. I'm not saying that you love your family any less. I'm saying that your hunger for what you were born to do *will grow*. You'll figure out how to answer the call, or you'll stifle it. Trust me! You can do both. You can be a great mom and a dream chaser!

We all have talents, gifts, and resources to give away to our family, friends, and the world. We all have a unique voice that must be shared. When I say *voice*, I mean your specific way to express who you are. You have to find yours. Your kids are not the sum total of you. Let me say that again: your kids are not the sum total of you. I know there are people who say we single parents should focus on our kids and let who we are sit and simmer on the back burner of our lives. But listen, we have so many examples of single parents doing it today. There's no reason to think that you and I can't be who we are *and* parent well also.

I can hear you now: "But I don't have a special talent. I wasn't made to be great." Or maybe you say, "I don't know what my purpose is." Sound familiar? I know it does because I was once in that very position. I know what it is to ask, "Why am I here, Lord?" or "What is my talent?" The truth is we all come to some point where we want the answers to these questions—and rightly so. We know there is greater for us. We all secretly know how awesome we are and seek to show that awesomeness to the world. The question then becomes in what stage and how?

The Point of it all/Stick with Me

When I was little, all my family (or at least it seemed like it was my whole family) knew how to sing. I wanted to sing like them, but instead of using my own style and gifts, I mimicked the stronger voices and tried to sing hard and tough like the rest. I was a mezzo-soprano and loved all things soprano. I loved ranges, really. Unfortunately though, I tried to be all of them instead of what I was. Subsequently, I ruined my voice and trained my throat that high notes should be left to Mariah Carey. My point? We have to be ourselves and operate in our why. I can't be you and you can't be me. But…

we can be powerful in our own way.

You may not feel it or even think you do, but we all have a *purpose*. We all have gifts on the inside that must be used for our good and the good of others around us. You just have to find out what that is for you. I call that "finding your why." We've all seen people we want to emulate. They seem to have it all together and are experts at what they do, whether that be connecting, serving, networking, speaking, etc. They're happy, fulfilled, and excited about what they're doing. What's so special about these people? They simply have zeroed in on their *why*. That's what I want for you and every woman I can touch. That, my friends, is my why- to help you move closer to yours.

Let me tell you my truth. Having a family does not stop the burn in our hearts to achieve our dreams. I know. I felt guilty for wanting to do it all, have it all, see it all, etc. And I've talked to enough women to know that guilt is there. For some reason, if we work (and we need to as single moms), we feel guilty for not being the stay-at-home mom we dreamed we'd be—or at least I did. And instead of celebrating how awesome we are to be able to provide, we are sad that we're not spending as much time as we'd like. Let it go, sis! The guilt must go.

Now what I'm about to say may be totally opposite of what some folks will tell you. Listen anyway. Being content raising your kids while putting yourself on the back burner sounds selfless and wonderful, but it will kill your joy, your spirit, and your zeal for life. Being a single mom is surely not what most of us thought we would be, yet we are. I want you to know that being a mom is a calling, a gift, a blessing, but life doesn't stop there. It doesn't stop because we became parents. It may be harder to do what we had originally planned, but it's not impossible.

Hear me good. I'm not saying that choosing to focus solely on your kids is wrong. If that's for you, by all means do it, but you'll still yearn to complete your original goals. Yes, some women have been able to say good-bye to their dreams. I'm not one of them. I'm not able to make peace with being a single mom that lives in the background of my children's lives, and you don't have to be either! I'm too fabulous to lie dormant. And guess what—so are you. Somebody needs my gifts! And they need yours, too. *You just have to find your why, develop the balls to chase it, and do it anyway!* Yep! I said grow some *cojones.* (I know. I'm sassy!) Are you really content staying on the sidelines until your kids are eighteen? Nah! Not me! We gone do this thing together. They're going to get the best mom who loves them and also rocks her dreams. Talk about leaving a legacy!

Why Now

The time to come out of the stagnant, can't stay balanced with it all, overwhelmed state you are in … is now! It's time to truly live. An invigorated, happy you is an invigorated, happy family. When you walk in your purpose, do you know how that really translates for your kids? They get a happy mom. They get a mom who doesn't regret being where she is. They get a mom who is showing them how to roll with life and come out a winner. Ah! No one has ever said it that way, have they? Nope! But that doesn't make it less true. Choosing to not chase your dreams is hurting your kids more than you think. Let's face it. I see far too many single moms complaining instead of celebrating. It's rough. I agree. Been there. Bought the T-shirt and the mug. But it's not impossible to do. Your kids are waiting for the real you to stand up. Will you give them the real you? Will you give the world the real you—your gifts, time, talent, and expertise?

Someone is waiting on you to walk in your purpose. They need your gifts to be who they are called to be.

Now that you're a parent, has your "why" changed? Do you still feel passionate about what you were doing, or has having your babies opened you up to a whole new world of experiences? Hmm? If so, it's time to find your *next* "why". Hopefully your mental juices are flowing now. See, I believe we all have a purpose to fulfill and that as we move along, sometimes that purpose changes. Think of it like this: You were a cheerleader in high school. You also loved God and behaved like someone who did. You treated everyone well (not just the cool kids). Your purpose in that season was to show other girls (who never got picked for the squad) how to make the team and share Jesus or rather how to use the space you're in to be a light. Then you graduated and moved on to college. Now you're not pursuing cheerleading, but you are still sharing your faith as a member of the student council because being a cheerleader helped you get rid of your shyness, and it gave you boldness and an "in" to speak to those who normally wouldn't listen. Do you see in this example how your position changed throughout life but your purpose stayed the same and moved with you as you went into different arenas?

Sometimes, it's only in looking back that we can really see why things happened.

In my life, I look back and count my bad days as good. I can now see how they were leading me to my purpose. What do you see when you look back? Has your purpose changed? Is parenting enough for you right now, or do you long for more? No pressure. Just think on it.

As cute and as special as your kids are, that, my friend, will not calm the desire for success and achievement you have within yourself. It must be answered. It must be *quenched*. You just have to find your why. What is it you were made to do? What makes you smile and gets you geeked up at the sheer mention of its name? Hmm? *That*, sweet sister, is your *purpose*.

I heard a popular radio host say something so crazy years ago that it caught me by surprise and I had to pull over. She said that if women get divorced, they should not date or remarry. They should just focus on their kids. I thought that was just ludicrous. She said they should focus only on the kids until the kids graduate. Well, that sounds great for her. She was married, she had a smooth life without the problems she mentioned, and she hadn't experienced that same situation at all. It just doesn't make sense. You do not put your life on hold, no matter how awesome it sounds to be so selfless that you in essence starve yourself to feed the kids. Child, please! She obviously hasn't been home alone with her kids in a while because the two I got are awesome, but they drive me bonkers, wonkers, and everything in between after a couple hours! And I do the same to them!

Listen, sis, let's keep it very honest, very real. You are a woman. You have needs. You cannot wait five to ten years to fill those needs. That makes you angry and ruins your kids' childhood. Do you really want to hear them say "Mommy is an angry "nut basket" because she needs a man." No one should forego human interaction period. No one should forego living their best life for any reason single mom or not. No one should forego having what *they* need and doing what they must at the same time. The universe is big enough, and there are plenty of people looking for what you have. You can't meet them, however, if you're spending all your time in the house. Girl, get up, get out, and live.

So it's clear you ache for something greater or you wouldn't be reading this book. It's clear you also believe, like me, that you can raise great children, give them what they need to thrive, AND have a healthy, fulfilled life at the same time. So how do you get there? You get there by doing some soul-searching. I know. What a fancy term for such a hard process. But search you must. Your why is tied up in who you are. No one can tell you what it is but you, and you already know what it is. It's what you often dream about doing if you had enough of this or enough of that. It's what you wake up dreaming about. It's on your mind when you lie down. It's what you talk about every chance you get. It's what you're too afraid to do. It's the *why* you were born and the *what* you need to do to be satisfied.

All I'm discussing here is your purpose. The "why am I here?" question is all about our design by God to do something great in the Earth. To get to the final answer, *which I really think we all know already*, you just go through the process. Don't fight it. Your process is that feeling of your stomach turning inside out which plays out over different scenarios until you get to a place of total acceptance and peace about the move you should make. This will take time. How much? I have no idea. That, my sister, is between you and God. But what I can offer you are some stages and steps. Read on.

Step 1: Let go of the fear of knowing it all.

There's no way you'll know it all, which isn't bad. Sometimes we wouldn't take the leap of faith it takes to get to our destiny if we knew all about the drama, pain, joy, defeat, failure, mishaps, unexpected setbacks, etc. in between. We'd run for the hills if we knew the struggle was *really* real. But God shows us the end, and the end is so glorious—scary to grasp that it can be ours but exciting to pursue. You get it. It's a bag full of emotions. But take the plunge we must, or we'll have to live with the pain of never trying. Who wants that?

So, give up the reins. You won't be leading this ride. To get to your why, you have to relinquish control over everything and let life do as it does—surprise you. Still not convinced? Well, let me tell you a story.

Before I moved states (for the most part), I was in a good place in my life, I had moved on but I had no co-parenting help from my kids' dad, and that bothered me. I had a job and a place to stay, and my kids were healthy. But, I had no "me time" retreat. I was *on* ALL THE TIME. As you know, when children are small, they require so much more than when they're teens. Real talk, I just needed a break. I was spent and pushing through on fumes of the greatness I possessed. He wouldn't help, and we lived in the same city. Yes, I know. Blank stare inserted. But, you better know that nothing can stop your greatness. There is always another way!

As providence would have it, I began to grow and chase my dreams. Doing that opened me up to people who would support me and help me get those outlets I needed. A job opportunity arose. I took it. That changed my life because it gave me a new environment. Remember, my first job was full of drama. As I began to move in my purpose, a door I wasn't expecting opened. See now why you must move in yours?

As you know another job came up, and this time it was out of state. Like I've already told you, I took that, too. It was scary to even think of moving to a place where I had no family or friends with a four-year-old and a six-year-old. But I surprisingly had so much peace about it. I prayed and I felt God telling me to take the plunge. I did, and I haven't looked back since. In fact, I've been blessed beyond my wildest dreams to do what I do and to go where I've gone. The point is that I was scared, too. I had my doubts, too. But *I did it anyway*! And, my sister, you'll have to do just that in order to have what you say you want. No fear. Just faith. Take the plunge. When your door opens, walk through it.

Step 2: Move

I know I just turned your world upside down, but somebody had to do it. By all means, stay put if you are not feeling life's tug to move. If your life is great, this section is not for you. But if you know there's more, and you're not doing it, these are the cons you potentially face by not moving.

One, the longer you wait, the longer it will take. As the old adage goes, "Time waits for no man," so don't wait too long to seize your day. You can still do it. Yes, you can. But it could take longer. Only you know what's right for you and your family. Assess your situation and plan for it. Change is tough, but sometimes it's necessary.

Two, you lose momentum. Look around you. How many people have shared a goal or dream with you only to let it fizzle by the wayside? When your dreams are calling you, chase them. As I've said, rising early and going to bed late are great indicators that you ought to look into what is nagging you to pursue it. Purpose is a pusher. What's occupying your time? What makes you get up early and go to bed late? You can't lie down on it. You've got to move!

Step 3: Take drastic measures.

Now, you may not have to move to another state like I did. Maybe you have to cut some things or people out of your big picture, make more time for this pursuit toward destiny, adjust your mindset around what you can actually have, etc. Let me tell you ... *Do It Anyway!* To have the life you want, you must be willing to do the work. To enjoy that vision you see in your mind's eye requires the work in the middle that no one tells you is going to be hard, grueling and worth it. Be willing to remove what's blocking your space and your dreams so you can have it. Take drastic measures to have what you know you can have. You and your children deserve that and more!

Step 4: Seek new sources of creativity.

In finding your purpose, your why, your thing, you may have to seek new sources of creativity—new music, new hobbies. You may have to release some things and/or people as I said. Look, a new life requires change. Only when you seek the *new* will you find what it is that you need. Be open to it. What you seek is seeking you as a popular quote goes. But I say, "What is for you you IS for you." Go get it, sis! Why not try something new? Read on to find out how.

Step 5: Try something new.

A renewed sense of purpose will have you trying new things, meeting new people, and increasing your social IQ. Allow it to do just that! After all, to make your dreams a reality, you will need a team and in chasing your purpose, your team will come.

Trying something new can be scary and invigorating. I'm the resident introverted extrovert (air quotes), so I know scary. But, I'm also an oxymoron in that I refuse to back down from a challenge. Basically, I refuse to lose. So, my not chasing a dream or completing a goal feels like I've been challenged to defend my honor, yet I cowered in defeat. I can't have that. No ma'am, that's not okay with me. I want you to be that tenacious about your purpose. Refuse to be okay with never knowing what it's like to pursue your God-given why. Instead, chase it, run after it, and seize it!

Speaking about trying something new, I'm reminded of my first trip alone to a conference. I had the most fun and met people who are now a part of my row. But, going there alone, I had all types of made up ideas. None of which I ever saw. I'm forever connected to the men and women I met there and owe a great debt of gratitude to the presenters. It was amazing.

Now, imagine what and where I would be had I let fear keep me home. Try something new today! Be wise, but try it as it connects to your why.

Your purpose lies just outside your comfort zone.

It takes discomfort to birth world-class athletes, pianists, doctors, etc. All these giants in their fields that we see and admire were, at some point, just like you and me. They were scared. But what they did, we need to do. They persevered, kept going when it got tough, and used the process to make them stronger. Now, they can be down 20 points in a game and come back. Why? Because they've been there before. They know what being down feels like and they know what overcoming a setback feels like. They picked up a strategy to win when everything is against them. Are you allowing your process to lead you to your why and to make you stronger?

Step 6: Help somebody else.

Still not sure what your why is? Help someone with theirs. In the process of serving, you'll begin to have ideas, extensions of ideas, and gain an overall sense of accomplishment. It's also a good time to just release the questions about your purpose and do more for someone else. But know this: Nothing will happen until you make a move. Nada. If you are saying there isn't any tug on your heart to do more for you right now, then move where you feel life calling you to go higher. Move toward destiny. Destiny doesn't shout to us and say "Here I am! Let's change your life." No, it happens over time as you continue to move toward your next level. Only you know what that is. Help others and in the process, you will help yourself.

Life could be calling you to do something with your family. I love to get my boys involved in what I'm doing. So, be open to pursue your purpose along with your kids. You never know what awaits you on the other side of *yes* to destiny. Remember that waiting to be fulfilled isn't a strategy. Stepping up to the plate and swinging at the ball, now that's a strategy.

Whatever you do, find your why and chase it!

Action Steps: Soul-Searching Work

Step 1: To find your why, you have got to carve out time to think. Please understand that purpose is fluid. It changes. You'll know it when it calls you. Keep praying and asking God for direction. You have to be willing to confront every fear, every "what if," and every naysayer to have what you say you want. So do the mental and emotional work before you release your dreams to others. This is *your* life. You call the shots. You work for yourself and your babies. Let that sink in.

Step 2: Be real honest. Is what you have in mind a call on your life or just a wish?
This is the hard part that takes time. I know I said waiting can be a deterrent, but in this instance, I'm asking you to assess before you leap. Once you're

honest with yourself, you can get clear on how you'll begin this journey. And it is a journey. Make no mistake about it: you'll have to push through some t

things to possess your purpose, but it will be worth it.

Step 3: Make a list of the pros and cons for YOUR benefit.

Step 4: Pray about it all.
You may or may not have the same faith as me, and that's okay. I know that my faith has kept me through some storms, and as I have stepped out on faith (to the non-person of faith it looks like I blindly chased a dream), God has always made a way. In my own life, I have to pray about my decisions. If I don't receive peace about a thing, I don't do it. So I encourage you to give yourself some time to self-reflect without making brash decisions. Yes honey, that fiasco with my kids' dad brought me closer to God, grew me up, and now I use my common sense. When I don't have peace, I don't do it. I PRAY!

But let's assume you do have the desire to improve, grow, and go in the direction of purpose, you know what it is, and *you are ready*. Then sis, you should get to moving. Assess it all. No brash moves. Plot your course because you have a family to think about. And if you need help, I'm only a website click away at KaywandaLamb.com. After all, I'm The Single Mom Coach for a reason. And, I want you to SOAR! Yet I want you to develop a strategy to chase your purpose.

This is not a "quit your job tomorrow" pep talk. This is a "please look closely at your life and figure out what's missing" call to action.
Answer all these below in the notes section. Revisit this section often as you grow and go toward your purpose.

Question to ponder: What would make you live like you were intended? Hmm? How can you be impactful, grateful, magnetic, and purposeful?

_____

_____

_____

_____

_____

_____

_____

_____

_____

_____

_____

_____

_____

_____

_____

_____

_____

_____

_____

_____

_____

_____

_____

_____

_____

_____

_____

_____

_____

_____

_____

_____

_____

Do It Anyway!

STEP 3: FIND YOUR TRIBE

PART I

I know I had you doing deep soul-searching in chapters 1 and 2, but it ain't ova! Know this: It may not be easy to do the work we need, but it's worth it. In this chapter, I want you to remove the constraints, ideas, ideologies, and misconceptions about who your "tribe" is. I want you to be open to *new people* that love on you, your babies, *and* your dreams.

What do I mean by *tribe*? Well, Seth Godin (a hugely famous author who writes on business) says that a *tribe* is a "group of people connected to a leader, an idea and one another." They look to hear what you have to say, and they're your supporters. You're the leader/chief of sorts, and they (your tribe) wait to hear what you, *the Chieftain*, have to say. Isn't that awesome? I have some folks whom I will stop and drop everything to listen to. That's a privilege that I know they appreciate. I, too, have people who feel the same about me. I appreciate them, but they *are not* my tribe. They are my fans and I love them.

I take a very different view on this word *tribe*. A tribe, in my opinion, is very different from the above definition. For me, a *tribe* is a group of women and/or men that surround you and support you in *every area* of your life. You need a tribe. I want you to have a tribe. Let me show you how to find and build your own. See, as a single mom, you are going to need people that get you, support you, and have your back. Many of us don't live near family and that requires us to form new bonds and connections. How do you do that? Read on.

To be a part of a tribe, be willing to be vulnerable.

Be selective.

There's a phrase I use all the time. I didn't create it, but it makes so much sense. It goes like this: "Everybody can't go." Short and sweet. It may step on some folks' toes, but it removes chaos and adds peace to your life. Peace is a precious commodity. You have to be selective about whom you allow in your circle. Truth be told, we hold on to people who we know are not good for us. We try to love them in spite of their messiness or their bad attitude or even in spite of the fact that they're just not that into us. We do all of this, holding on to folks *who do not lift a finger to hold on to us*. But when the fire heats up in life and you call on these "place holders" to help you and they don't, you'll find it easy to cut your losses and walk away. It's a sad truth, but we all experience seasons where friendships we thought were rock solid ended. Instead of mourning them, we must learn to get glad. They made room for your tribe.

So, tell me! What's easier to walk away from? A job, friends, or what you thought was your life's purpose? When you find yourself in a situation where you're unhappy, unfulfilled, and stagnant, you will find a way to move! Not being surrounded by the right people to push you into your purpose simply causes you to suffer longer than necessary. Yes, you will suffer in mediocrity, trying to do things by yourself because you have no help. But, when you find your tribe, they will help you chase your dreams and your purpose better and faster.

To have a tribe, everyone can't go where you're going, so they can't be in your circle. Release them.

Be protective.

I've had my share of fake friends. You know … the kind that said they would but didn't. They said they were my friends, but they weren't there when I needed them. I've learned that the word *friend* is not one to be given to just anybody. It must be earned.

There's an old saying: "When people show you who they are, believe them." You have got to learn to release people who are not committed to you. These could be people related to you, but remember, everybody can't go. Let me tell you, if I don't know how to do anything else, I can release people from my life! Name it, and I've probably experienced it if it has to do with women, men, dating, business, coworkers, etc. I know what heartache feels like. I know what it's like to lose a good friend. And, I know what it's like to let go and live a peaceful life. Release people who are not for you, your success, and your purpose.

If they can let go of you, you must let go of them.

As it relates to getting to know new people. I know it can be hard. But, you must learn to let someone in. Be selective. Be on the lookout for self-serving folks. Chile, I've learned every nice person that swarms around you won't always be so nice and may never have been there for you in the first place. But you know what? I don't let that stop me from making new friends. I—you guessed it!—*Do it anyway!*

So as you build new friendships and connections, be wary of what people want from you in return. Be protective of the value you bring as someone's *friend*. They're gaining an invaluable asset when they gain you. Remember that!

To be wise in tribe building, you need to be vigilant. Know your worth and watch whom you let into your circle.

Be diligent.

Sometimes it takes a while to find out who's really in your corner. We all know how relationships go, so you may have to have a few bridges burned in your life to recognize your tribe. Don't give up. Actively seek to find them, to connect with them, to know them. These people will be your five most influential friends, business associates, or a mix of the two. You'll know them when you see them because they'll share the same hunger and spirit as you. They desire to make a difference, improve something, and solve a problem. Just like you.

Don't give up if you feel like you're all alone. I'm a witness people come to you at just the right moments in life. For example, I've recently added new members to my tribe after meeting some ladies at conferences over the last year, and it feels like we've known each other a lifetime! I was diligent. I looked for people who wanted what I wanted and had good hearts. It was no coincidence that we met and connected because people who share the same spirit of generosity usually find each other. I did pray for my tribe to come. But in my diligence and desire for "purpose" teammates, I also made sure to serve others who needed me.

One way to get closer to finding your tribe is through service to others. No one shows up and says, "Hey! God sent me to you." No. They show up and you get to know each other, learn about each other, and gradually get closer and release more information. It takes time to develop relationships that stick, that bind, that make your heart leap. But they happen all the time. Be diligent. They will come.

To be surrounded by those that root for you, be the first to root for someone else.

Pray about it.

Depending on what you believe, I'd recommend doing this every time you have a business or personal venture. You always want to make sure you're making the right move. Because I've spent time with people who didn't have my best interest in mind, I really want to make sure I don't do that again. I want the same for you. So take time to get still and pray for direction. Sometimes opportunities present themselves and it looks like the friendship would be a great idea. Hold off on rash decisions and check the fruit meaning check to see their motives. Pray and proceed.

As I was going into my new season as an entrepreneur in the online space and beyond, I prayed about God sending me people who were *for* me. *I had had enough of wasting my time, my energy, my peace, and my life in places where I didn't fit and with people who didn't fit my life.* Truth be told, they were never meant to walk this walk with me. THIS time, I wanted better. What are you wanting? Ponder it. Prepare for it. Wait on it.

Expect what you are praying for! Help God out by believing it can happen!

Just as people have come and gone in my life, I want to mention that many people will come into your life. Not everyone will stay. Even if they're a part of your tribe and you both work well together, life may take them in a different direction. That's okay. I believe God will always send you what you need. I also believe you have to have your eyes open to see your tribe for who they are. Who's in your life right now, divinely placed to help you go to your next level? Take some time and nurture that relationship. Not only nurture it, but *add to it*. It's worth it! Just like you need a tribe, they do too!

Get God involved in your dreams. He can bring a group of people that will help build the Ark of your life.

Be the tribe.

There is a popular quote by Paulo Coelho that says, "And, when you want something, all the universe conspires in helping you to achieve it" (*The Alchemist*). So as you move into your purpose, I want you to know that the people you seek are seeking you. All you have to do is keep moving toward your greater whether that be your greater purpose, relationship, goals, or your best self.

In the South we have a saying: "You can get more flies with honey." I want to insert that here because you can make more friends when you're friendly. Yes, I want you to smile and be open to the love *and* friendships that are coming your way. I know ... if your situation is anything like mine was (in those early years), *smiling* can be hard. But you gotta do it. And the truth is, the more you smile, the more your situation changes. There's something about a smile. It invites people to you. It's a signal that it's okay to approach. If you're too shy to make new friends, just go to new places and conferences and smile. The people you meet will do the rest.

So what am I asking you to do? I'm asking you to get uncomfortable and go meet new people. I'm asking you to be the awesome, helpful person *NOW* that you want to come your way. I'm asking you to be a tribe member for someone else *before* your tribe comes.

I put this in the book because many women have contacted me online saying the same thing: "I don't have any support where I live. I love your message. Why don't you build a forum for us, Kaywanda?"

My reply? "Until I do, you be the person you want to connect with." This section is designed to prod you out of your comfort zone and move you into being a tribe builder. It's scary to reach out to people, to be vulnerable, and to admit we *need* someone else. *Do It Anyway!*

I want you to begin being a place where other women can find connection, support, and peace of mind.

Being the tribe is all about not waiting on the cavalry to save you, to invite you into their group, to come along and help you get out of your comfort zone. None of that! It's about you *Doing It Anyway!* by yourself. You're strong enough, smart enough, and awesome enough to do this without the help of others. I want you to *own your awesome.* Your unique brand of awesome is wrapped up in your personality, your attitude, your skills, talents, and all that makes you...well, you. Use the steps below to find and build your tribe. NOW.

Action Steps:

1. Get vulnerable.
2. Be selective.
3. Be protective of yourself and others in your tribe.
4. Serve others.
5. Be diligent and look for opportunities to connect and be connected.
6. Pray about it all.
7. Be what you seek.

In the space below, write out your plan to build your tribe. Who are your current tribe members? Who do you want to add? Why?

_____

_____

_____

_____

_____

_____

_____

_____

_____

_____

_____

_____

_____

_____

_____

_____

_____

_____

_____

_____

_____
_____
_____
_____
_____
_____
_____
_____
_____
_____
_____
_____
_____
_____
_____
_____
_____
_____
_____
_____
_____
_____
_____
_____
_____
_____

Together we all win –Michelle Y. Talbert

PART II

Your kids need a tribe all their own.

You aren't the only one that needs a tribe. Your kids need a tribe. Make sure as you're forming connections (personal and business), that you're paying close attention to who might be great mentors for your kids. I say this because my boys have greatly benefited from having mentors. Right now, my boys are a part of a nonprofit called Project SOAR. It's based in Dallas, and only four boys participate in it at the moment, but it is poised to grow more and I want every single mom to have an organization like this. Each boy has two to three mentors. I love it! My boys have gone on job-shadowing trips, road trips to football games, college visits, and more because I've looked for good men to stand in the gap for them. That's what we must do in the absence of their biological dad, we must place good men around our boys who are committed to helping them soar. We must do the same for our daughters.

Don't feel bad if your kids don't have mentors though. Begin looking for people who can help you guide them into the next level of their lives. Not only do we as adults need to heal, find our purpose, and move in it, but so do our kids. *Let it be said that we did our best to get them to where they want to go.*

Please know that I didn't always have this much sense! I learned a lot along the way, and now I'm teaching you and every mama I can about how to make it as a single mom. Use the tips below to reach out to mentors for your kids.

What to Look for in a Mentor

1. Look for men and women you trust with your kids.
2. Look for men and women who have a stellar work ethic and a stellar reputation for putting *their family first.*
3. Look for people who can give your kids a window into a **better** world, a leg up in the workforce (great men and women in business, or those who are retired and love sharing their knowledge and time with young folks).
4. Look for people who already want to be mentors.
5. Vet the people you pick. Ask around about them. Create your own questions to ask them.
6. Ask your kids, if they are old enough, what they would like to have in a mentor.
7. Keep your eyes open. You never know what uncle, brother, cousin, neighbor, husband of a friend, boss, or coworker will come to your side and help you raise your children.

If you have boys, get male mentors. If you have girls, get female mentors. I know it's obvious about why you should pick like mentors. As they age, you can get a mixed group. But let me just say this: Even when we trust people, we ought to be cautious about who is pouring into our children. I did say find great mentors doing it in their field, but your kids' safety and the values you teach them at home should be of utmost concern.

Why is a mentor important?

As I said, your kids also have purpose. God has a plan for them, too. Part of their story is their time with you. Give your children all you got and then go get more! Provide what you can, and then surround them with good mentors so that they can grow up and be the great leaders God destined them to be!

Let's be honest. I'm a girl. I can do my very best, but even then I cannot teach boys to be men. I can teach them to be good human beings, but there's just some stuff I don't know. If you're in the same situation, you know how I feel.

This precise uneasiness about raising a boy is why I started seeking out mentors for my boys. My boys now have many mentors, but the first mentor outside of my relatives was my girlfriend Alys' husband, Justin.

After knowing them a few years, I got bold and asked her husband, Justin, to spend time with the boys. I had been watching him with his own kids, and I knew he would be perfect to mentor my boys. He only had girls, so he was geeked about it, but of course nervous too. It worked out, and to this day, he enjoys them and they him. My point? You never know if they will say yes, so ask away! Most people are waiting to share what they know and have learned with others.

Until Help Comes

It's important to say that you're doing a great job raising a family alone. I don't think we stop and celebrate how amazing it is that we didn't quit when life happened, that we kept going alone, and that our kids have love and their needs met. That's a blessing, and it deserves to be acknowledged. Woo!

Can you imagine how much extra help a good mentor will be to you and your kids? They can help them stay on top of homework, check in with them a few times a week, take them on outings, and give you a break (Haleluyurr!), etc. It's amazing what a great mentor can do for them *and you*. So, yes, your kids can benefit from mentors. I hope you're able to locate good men and women that will come alongside you and your kids and help you with the load.

But hear me good: If you don't find mentors soon—or ever—a dedicated mama that gives her 100% will always beat anything anyone else can do! Mentors aren't replacing you. They're assisting you in your purpose to grow up awesome young men and women.

Surrounding yourself with good people who support you and your kids is a must. On the road to your best life, you and your children will get exactly who and what you need!

Until help comes, *you be the change for you and your kids*. **I have faith in you. I know you can do it.**

What can you do to build relationships for yourself? How can you get people around you to support you and your kids? Who can help?

_____

_____

_____

_____

_____

_____

_____

_____

_____

_____

_____

_____

_____

_____

_____

_____

Your people are waiting. Go get 'em!

STEP 4: CONNECT WITH YOUR KIDS

Yes, this is a necessary part of the puzzle. Connection is what family is all about. Some of my fondest memories are of me and my family growing up in Louisiana. I can still picture how my grandparents led our family with strong resolve and love. I remember how they kept everyone coming home for what seemed like every holiday. Life was about family. Family was everything. And for me, it still is. However, it wasn't always a bed of roses for me as a young parent. I had my *stuff*. As you saw in Step 1, I had some issues to get over. Chile, didn't I! And although I loved my babies and did the best I could, some days I was just *getting by*. Real talk, there were some days where it was all I could do to get us fed, work, and get from A to B. Surviving. Not my best life. Read on to figure out how to get out of that place and CONNECT with your kids!

The Not So Pretty

I don't know about you, but I struggled at times to stay fully connected to my young boys. Now, I was there, I was providing, but something was missing. I loved them and I'm sure they didn't notice my struggle to get it all done. But in my mind I was battling to be the perfect mommy that I thought I should be to them and at the same time, battling the reality of my overwhelm. But although I was beat down by life, tired, and hurting, I knew I wasn't *fully* present. If that's you, there's no shame in that. I want to say to you to come out of that funk and connect. Now. You can do this. You *have* to do this for your family.

Now, there are people who never disconnected from their kids, but they also never connected in the first place. Let's be honest. Folks have gotten pregnant for various reasons, and not all of them have been planned. I see women like this all the time. They provide food and shelter but aren't involved in day-to-day life with the kids. They may even have lots of money, but the kids are missing that human connection they dream about and read about in magazines. Let's not seek perfection in our parenting. But, let's seek to be the best parent we can be. This is why I wanted you to heal first. As I went through my healing process, I was able to focus more on me and my boys and, more importantly, on *our* connection. We must seek connection with our babies. We know what happens when kids don't get the love and support they need. I don't know about you, but I'm not about to let my boys go off into the world with less love, time, and affection than I can give.

DO IT ANYWAY

We need to be the place of solace for our kids.

As a young, stressed out, single mom that had two babies to raise, I never told my doctor what I was feeling. I can see now that I probably should have. Heck, it could've been exhaustion. It could've just been mom guilt. But I'm being honest when I say that I know *I wasn't fully living* up to parenting the way I am now. If that's you, prayerfully consider if it's something you need to talk to your doctor about, or if you just need a break. Either way, do the work and get what you need.

Some days, I did all I could, and then I went to sleep. Ha-ha! We all took naps together back then. They were tiny tikes. Honey, I was whipped. I did what I could, and some days they got more than others. I realized I was sleep walking my way through life. That's why I write to ask you not to sleepwalk your life away. No more routine parenting! Be present.

I'm so fervent in asking you to release whatever has you bound and down, whipped and possibly exhausted. Our kids need us so that they can learn to love, grow, and do their best in life. We're the examples. We can get so busy providing and repeating the same old routine that we forget to fully live. That's not what I want for you. I want you to connect! Be present! Live! I know it's hard, but you gotta do it, mama. They're depending on you to show them how good life can be, even *if* somebody has walked away. Even *if* it's just you and them against the world. Even if … Insert what you want, but you must connect and show your children that thriving is exactly what you will do!

Get the picture? I'm not saying don't rest. I'm saying prepare to be connected to your babies. Just like a good basketball player comes off the bench, gets in the game, and takes his team to the win, I want you to get in there and parent. We don't need to assume life will be perfect once you begin connecting. *But I guarantee you that you're perfect for them, and they're perfect for you.* Connect and watch your relationship improve. They want the real you, and I know you want to show your "awesome" not only at work and with your friends or in the community, but also with your kids.

Rise up! It's your time to be able to pursue your purpose, chase your dreams, and lead your family.

Find time to talk.

I make my boys put all electronics down during breakfast, lunch, and dinner at home. Sometimes when we're out to dinner, I use some of that time to work, so I do let them vent using their devices. But the point here is not so much what they do, but what you all do when you make time to hang out. I want you to be very strategic in gathering information from them. Be sure to ask them questions (stealthily, of course) and really get to know how they work. I find that when I'm paying attention to them, they tell me everything I want and *need* to know.

This is a powerful tool to have in your arsenal, so make sure you train your kids that you're always going to want to know what's going on with them. Now, let me say this: They may not always want to talk to you. This is why you have to know what's going on with them, and finding time to talk helps you get the intel on their lives. Yes, you need to know their ins and outs—not like a hovering helicopter mom (don't do that) but as a mom who genuinely wants to know what's going on.

If they're having a bad day, someone hurt their feelings, or they're having a mood swing, etc., it may take a few tries to be able to talk to them. You've got to know when to give them space and come back later and when to keep digging. Your relationship with them will dictate how deep you go in your fact-finding. But please know that you're the parent, and you must get to the bottom of things. They may act like they don't want you to know, but deep down, they do. So pry and pry away!

Family Time

Family time will probably be something totally different for you and your kids, but for me and mine it's a chance to hang out and connect. Because I'm a busy entrepreneur, we usually do family time once a week. It entails takeout and a movie, or maybe we go to a movie. I've had some lean times over the years, and that can mean re-watching a movie we already own. The point is that we're together. My oldest acts like he wants it the least, but he's the main one asking about when we're having family time again! Right! He knows he needs connection.

Your kids always need you no matter how old they get.

What have you noticed in your kids? Are they asking for more time with you? Could it be that, by acting out in certain ways, they're showing you signs that the stuff—the provision—is nice, but can they please have some family time with you? If you think the answer is yes, make time today! It doesn't have to cost a lot or take a lot of time. But spending time with your kids will make your life easier in so many ways. I'm telling you from experience. You want to be proactive here and not reactive.

Take some time to brainstorm things you can do for your own special time with your kids. I have a girlfriend who has little separate dates with each of her boys. One thing I want to make sure I do is send them into the world ready. Spending time talking to them one-on-one helps us make sure we are pouring into them. I don't know about you, but I want my boys to become men with the wisdom and values I hold dear. I don't want them to grow into men with something they pick up along the way from people who don't care about them like I do.

See family time as your legacy, and you'll make time for it.

Sometimes you gotta get down and dirty.

I know you're busy. So am I! But our kids are our first job. Let that sink in. They're not *one* of our jobs. They're the *first*. And how well we do with them dictates how well, in some cases, they do. So I want parenting your babies to be at the forefront of your mind. Now, depending on how you became a single parent, you may have some issues with connecting with your babies. I want you to know that's okay. You know I had a few months where I didn't feel as close as I should have to my boys in those early years. Like I said, it was rough. I was making ends meet, and I was broken-hearted and my vision of our best life was cloudy. But I came up out of that, and if that's you, deal with it now. Talk to someone and keep connecting to your kids. Keep pushing for the relationship you know you all deserve to have.

Now, what do I mean about getting down and dirty? I mean doing stuff they want to do. Like I said, I know you're busy and you're concerned about meeting their needs and keeping a roof over their heads. But, listen to me good. They also *need* you. They need you to get in there and not just parent, but to be fun to live with while parenting. I call this distracting them when they're small and loving on them when they're bigger kiddos.

Little babies like to cut up. To halt that, I used to distract my boys by making them laugh, interrupting their hissy fits with play, etc., so I was distracting them by having fun with them. As the mom, you know when

they're just acting up or when they need food or cleaning. I could tell when mine were just utilizing what God gave them, so I'd use the brain he gave me and redirect them without them knowing it. I admit it: It was so much fun to see their little faces when they realized they had been tricked into having a good time instead of giving me a rough one. Try it! It works! I'm so good at this that my co-workers call me "The Baby Whisperer." Smiles and give self high-five. I learned in the struggle.

As my boys grew, I'd throw in a pillow fight every now and again. I'd take them out to throw the ball around or race them. I didn't want them missing out on anything that boys like to do because they didn't have a dad who was present. No, I knew how to do those things, so I did them. They still tell the story of how I fell throwing the football around with them and rolled down a hill (for what seemed like eternity). My feelings were so hurt after that fall, not to mention my bottom. But we still fall out laughing about it. Hey, I didn't say I was the best. I said, "I tried." I *did it anyway!* Do that kind of stuff with your kids. It builds memories and connections no one can take away.

With your big babies, you gotta love on them, too. Learn to speak their language. Get up and do some things they like. I can't stand video games, and I'm not interested in sweating unless I'm working out, but you know what? I do things I don't like because *they* like them. At thirty-eight years old, screaming at the top of my lungs on a Ferris wheel is embarrassing, but I do it anyway. Running around in a *hot* laser-tag suit is HOT, but I do it. (I win, by the way. That helps.) You see, I do these things and many more that they like because I want to build my connection with them. Our kids need to know we have their backs, that we are their support and not leave that up to someone outside our home.

They may have one parent, but the one they got is in it to win it!

The Game Plan

If you're rocking in this area, *go you!* We all are on a journey. Our jobs are to be as present as possible for the people that matter. If you need help in this area, seek it! Go get it! But please know that it's never too late to improve your relationship with your kids. Never.

Action Steps:

1. Assess your connection with your kids. Fix it if it needs doing. Improve it if that's what you need. Begin connecting if that's where you are. Just start.
2. Create moments for you and your kids. No set family time or one-on-one time? Take some time to brainstorm what you can do to build your connection. This book is all about you coming back to the "you" God made you to be. Part of you is your kids. As you grow and soar, so should they. You being your best you will help them be the best them they can be. Yaaas!
3. Implement your plans. Do what you need to make sure this happens often. Don't feel guilty if you miss a day. Make plans to enjoy each other. Just as you make time for every other area of your life, make time for your kids.

They will always remember the moments you shared. And keep in mind, your being there for them helps them to behave for you.

What ideas come to mind to start connecting with your kids today?

_____

_____

_____

_____

_____

_____

_____

_____

_____

_____

_____

_____

_____

_____

STEP 5: GET ORGANIZED

So you've learned that you need to heal in order to live. You've also learned that you need to find what gets you excited about life and thus what you should be doing for a living or for service to others—your *why*. You then moved on to building a strong link with your kids so that you can do all the above *and* know your handpicked, tried-and-true *tribe* is with you.

Now, in order to get the dream rolling, you've got to find clarity, get organized, and literally get your house in order. You know that if you have more than one child—or even just one—being a single parent can be chaotic. Lol! What is *clean*, anyway? But seriously, you've got to put systems in place to help you be successful. Trust me. I speak from experience.

Having a lack of control over the house, the kids, and you yourself breeds disorder. It breeds you being behind schedule, cranky, tired, and you being a *hot mess* basically. If that's you today, you need to fix that. When we're out of order in some area of our life, it affects another area. How do I know this? Well, I'm a woman and Mom guilt is real (I wish you could see the side-eye I gave mom guilt. But, I digress). I grew up in a clean environment. We were poor, but what we had we took care of. That makes me who I am—or it's part of it at least. So I view life and value things differently than a teenager who thinks food is to be dropped on the floor. Can you see me frown? How about now?

I jest (kind of), but I'm very serious about how our experiences affect our makeup and our makeup affects our mindset. If you are in clutter, then your thoughts are *not* flowing clearly. You may not want to be in clutter, but maybe you're overwhelmed. Or maybe you think this is the way life is supposed to be with small kids. It's not.

Now, I'm not talking about the state of your house exactly. Trust me. Mine can look like a tornado just went through it. I have smelly teens as well. What I'm getting at is that the house, the car, the job, the room, *that* room, etc. can cause you to feel stuck because you're too tired and busy to clean it, but it bothers you. Anything that bothers you or keeps you stuck from moving is a distraction.

You can beat distractions by facing them.

I have three solutions:

1. *Clean it up.* Whatever it is. If it's something emotional or mental, revisit chapter 1 because healing is key. Our inner world affects our outer world. Get your inside right.

2. *Pay someone else to clean it up.* If the house is driving you nuts and your schedule is that busy, you, sis, must find $50 and a maid. I know for some it's a luxury and an expense, but you gotta do it. If you can afford it, treat yourself. If it's not feasible, work overtime, do a side job, and/or request it as a birthday or holiday gift. It will bless your spirit and make more room for family time.

3. *Utilize the other people you already have in your house.* I have teens, so that means I don't wipe up behind them all day. They have chores. Like typical teens, they may miss a day or flat-out not do it. At that time, I reintroduce them to Kaywanda. *She don't play.* So if your kids are big enough to fix their own lunch, talk to girlfriends all night, and play video games, they're big enough to clean. Hand them the gloves.

Release the mom guilt.

Mom guilt is so real, but in this chapter I want you to get clear that it's had its last laugh in your life. Yes ma'am, mom guilt has got to go! Part of your gaining clarity is understanding that you're doing absolutely too much. Yes, too much! If there are areas in your life where people can help you and you aren't allowing them, stop that. Getting organized requires you to assess not just your physical space but also your mental space.

Releasing guilt is hard because you've been carrying it around for so long. But know this: You are not your past. You're growing and going. You're an amazing mom, and your kids bless you. That is the truth. Stop feeling guilty for forgetting to buy cupcakes or for the fact that your child has clean clothes but not new ones or for all the things we feel bad about and our kids never notice. Just release it all!

> *Getting over being perfect allows you to be who you were designed to be. That, sis, is awesome!*

Mom guilt oftentimes turns into feelings of being overwhelmed, and that is the *LAST* thing you need. I'm all about you living your best life. In order to have that, some feelings have got to go! Kick them to the curb. What do I mean? Well, have you ever had this scenario?

Your child tells you three weeks ahead of time that they have a project, but you forget about it. They have to put it together at the last minute, and they get a B! Oh no … not a B! They're mad. You suck for like 5 minutes until they forget about it and move on. Yes, mom guilt is real. Face it, you need systems in place so that you don't forget. But even if you do, it's not the end of the world. Trust me. You both will live. It may take a while for them to stop fuming, but it will be okay.

Now, what could help you avoid this scenario? A plan, a system, a strategy for living—ORGANIZATION. Yes! See, you know you need it. Let's find out how to do that.

Ways to get Organized Now

1.   *Visualize it.*

See the desired result in your mind and think about how you would feel if you had a clean house and/or a clean work area, if your week was planned out, if you knew ahead of time what your schedule looked like, etc. Organization is more than having a tidy home; it's having a tidy life. Organization will help you function better.

2.   *Use a planner.*

I love physical and online planners. I have a physical planner in the works for busy moms like me, and right now you can grab a free Get Organized template online at <u>KaywandaLamb.com/freeresources.</u>

Planners help you get your life! If you write it down, you can remember it. Now, there are levels to this, so don't move too fast. I don't want planning to overwhelm you. Planning out your week should allow you peace of mind and time to see where you can fit in the self-care you need.

I want you to set aside time to plan your life, your week, and your day. Sundays or early Saturday may work, but pick what you can do and start small.

3.   *Ask a friend to be your accountability partner.*

I love having friends keep me accountable. In fact, this is why most things get done because we have bosses looking for our productivity, we have kids looking for us to make the world go round—we have folks we are accountable to. So get a friend involved in keeping you organized. You'll be glad you did.

Now, ask yourself: "Do I really want my best life?" If you answered yes, then commit to doing the work to clear the clutter. Clutter comes in three forms: *mental, physical,* and *invisible.* Clutter goes deeper than stuff that takes up physical space. More often than not, a person who has excessive physical clutter is dealing with an emotional issue. Something has their attention to the point that they cannot clean.

Think of all the people you know with really cluttered homes. They're busy, got a lot going on, and/or they're dealing with something they can't let go of. Some people have medical issues and that keeps them from doing all they want. Yet others seem perfectly fine but are cluttered to the hilt. What makes a person disorganized? They haven't taken control of something that is controlling them. When you get that thing—whatever it is—under control, you'll crush it!

Now, I'm not calling your house dirty. If you have kids and your house is spotless, you're my hero because mine isn't. But if you have stuff in your space and you can't concentrate because of the clutter, move it. Get rid of it. Cleansing feels so good. Mental and physical clearing of your spaces from time to time will do you good. Get organized. A cluttered mind won't make the moves it needs. And is, it's your time to make moves!

Action Steps:

1.   What are you holding onto that you need to release? This could be physical, mental, or emotional.

2.   What is this thing or things doing for you?

3.   What would your life look like if it was organized, if you had a handle on your day-to-day, if you had order? I know you want this. Let's do the work.

4.   What steps *can you* take now to change it all?

5.   Do all the things you thought of to clear the physical, mental, and emotional clutter in your life. If it takes confronting some things or talking to someone, do it anyway!

Take some time and journal thoughts and a plan here:

_____

_____

_____

_____

_____

_____

_____

_____

_____

_____

_____

_____

_____

_____

_____

_____

_____

_____

_____

_____

_____

_____

_____

Having a plan will bless you.

STEP 6: GET FOCUSED

Why do I have this chapter right here? Simple. After you've decided to get over the crap in your life, once you're closer to figuring out your purpose and you and your kids are ready to take on the world, it's only right to get laser-focused on your goals. I want you to win. I say that a lot because I *so* mean it. Getting focused in every area of your life may sound hard, but it isn't. When you get tired of life being a certain way, you get serious about change. So, are you ready to change some things? Let's do it!

Mindset

What you believe about you and your goals is more important than the goals themselves. Hear me.

> *You won't achieve anything if you don't believe you can.*

So we need to delve a little bit into your beliefs around success. Success in your home and love life is just as important as your success at work. So many factors affect you and me and we don't even know it. All those stories people told us about ourselves have to be retold from *our* healed perspective. What do you think about that? Does that sound fair? Hang in here with me. I won't get too deep.

Let me give you an example. When I was young, I wanted to be a famous model or actress. However, my circumstances didn't line up with that. How would I audition? Did I really have the talent?

It takes money to do that! Who's going to take me? See? All those tapes were playing in my head. I never asked anyone to help me, and I never tried. I just assumed I wouldn't be able to do it. To have what you say you want, you've got to do some mental work to change the tapes—the messages, all the negative crud that is keeping you from soaring—that replay in your mind. We're going to discuss that in this chapter.

To move forward and change your mindset, I want you to do an exercise with me. Let's look at some goals you've set in the past. Did you accomplish them? Why or why not? Now, this isn't a test. It's an exercise for you to do so that you can see what your mindset was around this goal. As in my example above, my mindset kept me from doing something that I wanted simply because I couldn't *see* it. I've been able to do what my mind said I couldn't just this year- model. What if I had chased that dream then? Where could I be? Where would my family be? See why it's important to get our minds in line with our hearts? Read on.

Goals

You've heard this Zig Ziglar quote, I'm sure, but I'm gonna say it again: "If you aim at nothing, you will hit it every time." Wow! Right? So after reading this section, you're not only going to aim at your goals, you're going to achieve them! Let's talk a little about how to get from where you are right now to where you know you should be. You've got to continue with the mindset shift I was talking about, and you've got to now attach some goals to this new dream you see for yourself.

Example Goal: I want to raise great kids who go off to college and are prepared to succeed.

A good goal like the one above must be combined with a good strategy. Your strategy is the tactics you will use to get you to the end result.

Example Strategy: Parent all the time, even when it's hard. Enroll your kids in extra tutoring for college preparation. Research their chosen career paths early and check in with them on their academics and their dreams. Talk to the school counselor about their options and available scholarships. Apply for said scholarships. Tour a college campus, etc.

See how a goal is just the beginning, but a strategy gets you the end result? In this book, the focus is on YOU. Yes, your kids will be impacted and better for the work you do here, but the focus is on you. How do you see your life? How will you grab hold of what you know you are supposed to have? Strategy, my dear! Strategy!

Targets

As you look out over the next twenty years, what do you see? I want you to set benchmarks or targets for your life so that you will know your strategy is working. I'm an educator, so in my field, we have standardized tests. For our students to succeed on those tests, we give them benchmarks before the real test comes to assess where they are. We're looking for a couple things with a benchmark: (1) We want to know how the child is doing now, and (2) We want to check their progress from the last benchmark. Get my point? Set targets for you to hit like the expert goal setter you know you are. When you aim for success, you'll hit it every time.

Example target for you: I will be a better, more engaged mom.

Example strategy: Adjust your schedule. Build in more time for the kids. Build in family fun. Say "no" to some things so that you can say "yes" more often to the kids. Implement a set day for family time and stick to it. Ask the kids how they're doing and actually unplug from everything to listen, etc.

And remember, I'm no perfect mama. I get busy too and have to redirect myself. But if you know you're lacking in some areas, get yourself on a schedule to doing better. After all, we're parents for a season and then they grow up. Let's give them the best of us!

Assess yourself often to see if you're where you want to be.

Buy a planner if need be and plug in the time you want to be able to spend with your kids. Don't forget to plug in time for yourself too! Remember, it's all about balance.

How to Get Laser-Focused on Your Greater

It wasn't until I was sick and tired of crying over a man who didn't want me that I got serious about what on earth was next for my life. It wasn't until I got tired of making $26,000 a year that I moved on to figure out how to make more money and get more education. Notice a pattern? Yep, *I got tired.* You must get tired too in order to have the greater experiences, jobs, relationships, etc. that you know life has for you.

I want you to *come back* to the awesome you that you are. That's why I took the time to talk about your mindset and your goals. Once you know your purpose, you've got to go after it. So much is riding on you stepping into who you are. When you reach for your greater, your babies are blessed, you are blessed, and the people whom you are designed to reach will be blessed. You have to get laser-focused about your goals because if you read "Find Your Why," you know you aren't here just for you. So, how do you get laser-focused? Read on. Hint:

Focus on one thing.

Yep, your success lies in your ability to zero in on why you're here and to do just that. That may require you to limit your usual downtime, but if it's for your purpose, it's worth it. You may have to totally rearrange your work schedule. Do it. You may have to get less sleep. Do it. Purpose is so powerful it cannot wait. Your dreams are so powerful they cannot wait. You've got to see the urgency in being excellent, and that will give you the energy to focus on *your one thing*.

Now, I didn't say focus so much on your goals that you neglect others. No, it will take a plan, and now that you know where you're going and how to build that out by goal, strategy, and benchmark, you're on the road to success! I would be remiss if I told you it was going to be easy. It won't. But it will be worth it.

Say it with me: "My goals, plans, dreams, and desires are worthy. No matter what, I will do it anyway!"

Go be great! It's already in you.

Action Steps: End of Chapter Reflection

Wow! Are you fired up? I am! Woo! To help you plot your awesome goals, I want you to take your time and fill this section out. Give your dreams time. Don't rush through this process. This is a section that I want you to revisit often. You may change a goal, complete a goal, or delete it. But one thing is for sure: unless you commit to it, you will miss it every time. Commit to your improvement and your better life that awaits you. Read on to see how.

Reflection is something I've learned to do a lot of as a teacher, and it has become an excellent practice in my own life. Reflection is simply the act of looking back to learn from it. When we reflect on our parenting, on our relationships, on our careers, there's so much for us to learn. A wise woman will look to see where she can improve, yes. But she will also look back and be proud of what she's done.

I want you to journal some thoughts here about what you want to achieve and how you're going to get there. I also want you to reflect on what was good on your journey and what you will change. There's so much power in writing. It's my hope you'll learn to reflect often. When you're older and you look back on your writing, you'll be reminded of how much you've grown. Grow, sis! Grow! It looks good on you!

DO IT ANYWAY

What do I want?

_____

_____

_____

_____

_____

_____

_____

_____

How will I get there?

_____

_____

_____

_____

_____

_____

_____

_____

Why do I deserve to have it?

_____

_____

_____

_____

_____

_____

_____

What have I learned on my journey?

_____

_____

_____

_____

_____

_____

_____

Is there more for me to learn in this area?

_____

_____

_____

_____

_____

_____

Where have I improved?

_____

_____

_____

_____

_____

What is my date to accomplish my GOALS? Why?

_____

_____

_____

_____

_____

_____

_____

What will I give up to get to my greater?

_____

_____

_____

_____

_____

_____

_____

_____

Use this space to journal your thoughts and reflect:

_____

_____

_____

_____

_____

_____

STEP 7: CRUSH YOUR FEAR

Life is too short to be afraid to go after what you want.

Yes, you guessed it! I'm not into fear. Not one bit! Now, I do *feel* fear, but I push through it. Let me qualify that by saying there were some times in my life when I wasn't this neck-snapping, side-eye-throwing, bold, unafraid mama, but life's worst moments have made me brave. What's building your bravery right now? Whatever it is, there's a purpose in it. You'll come out better than you went in.

I know I got you all fired up last chapter, and I'm glad I did because you must know that just as soon as you get ready to soar, to leap, to chase your dreams, fear will come. I too had to deal with fear to get to where I am today. I learned this lesson very well.

Like I said, I wasn't always the "Girl, you better make him treat you right or walk away!" kind of lady. I used to be the shy, "too timid to speak," church girl that thought a good woman kept quiet and that her love would cover all. Humph! In what life? Right!

So, my point here is that you must learn to confront your fears and overcome them. I don't want you stuck in crazy situations too afraid to move on. I want you empowered to stand up for yourself and to move effortlessly into your *better!*

I want you so unafraid of fear that you would rather launch out on your own than stay in a negative situation.

I'm no superwoman, but I like to think I am! There are many things I have to do that make me sweat profusely. Don't think I'm never afraid—it's okay to be afraid. But know it's not okay to stay afraid.

When I have to give speeches (and I love presenting), sometimes I notice my voice may shake a little. You know what I do? I *do it anyway*! The fear subsides because I remind myself that I'm just as amazing as the people in the audience, and I deserve to be there. I have something to say, and people are going to be blessed by it.

Depending on what brings you fear, you may have to do this too! Some say, "Fake it to make it," and that may work, but I like to face the root of the issue. And let's face it: sometimes we tell ourselves lies that don't mirror our greatness. Don't live with "what if" and "maybe." Push through your fear and *Do It Anyway!*

This chapter is more about never backing down from a challenge in every area of your life than hiding behind some mental reminders when you have to speak.

Hear me good: Whatever fears you have right now are okay to have, but make sure you know they aren't greater than your ability to overcome them. To be able to crush your fear, you'll have to do the following:

1. Get around people who love and support you.
2. Challenge your fears when they arise.
3. Step *way* outside your comfort zone every time you get the chance and do the thing that scares you.
4. Decide that hiding behind fear is short-circuiting your impact.
5. Face it—them, him, her—whatever *it* is.

What's your fear story?

I refused to leave this lesson out of the book. Fear keeps women from progressing and growing. After you've gone through heartache or betrayal, it just paralyzes you. It's the truth. Hurting is no fun. But once you go through or circumvent your process, or in your case after reading this book, you'll be able to rise up and crush your fears. Woo!

If we had our way, we'd always choose sunny days with no pain, but the pain has a point. It has a *purpose*. Somehow, even after overcoming all that held us back, we still have some fear no one knows about. And truth be told, it haunts us. Why is that? My theory is … because we don't share it with our loved ones, it has the opportunity to grow larger than it really is.

What if you ousted your fears? What if you gave voice to your courage instead? This is what you must do. I know it's scary. I've been where you are, but the pain of staying stagnant was so great that I got up the courage to try. Trying turned into me doing it anyway. And thus, the lady you see today was birthed. But it takes courage. One thing I know about you is you are courageous. You're a single mom. You work. You parent for real. You're reading this book. Yep, you're courageous.

75

My fear story started long before I ever became a single mom. I was the one who couldn't date because my family was strict. (My mom had me young.) My fear was I'd end up like her. That may hurt her to say that, but my motivation was to avoid being a single mom who had a limited education because she got pregnant as a teen. My fear was I'd never know how to date or be able to pick a good guy because I had no experience. Sure enough, my fear came true for a season. I didn't voice that fear. I accepted it to be true though, and out of all the guys to pick from, look what happened.

Yes, I shared my ugly truth. Why would I do that? I did it because I want to see you free from the bondage of your ugly story. So what … you messed up! Now what are you going to do to make it right?

A story like mine would make most crumble in self-pity, but I recognize my family was working with the knowledge they had at the time. I was working with what I knew. Although the information was wrong, I have two right babies. I choose to release any fear or guilt and live my best life.

If you can say you had a similar experience, I want you to know you may have made a decision, but *that decision does not have to make or break you.* What will you do with what you have now? That's my question. And believe me, you have more than one choice. Fear is not an option. Stuck is not an option. Living in shame is not an option. Choose joy. Choose life. Choose the truth, which is that you can make it, have made it, and will make it. No more bondage to fear!

Don't spend too much time wallowing in the past. Seize your now.

I've long since learned to date better and to stand up for my worth. But I want you to know you aren't alone. The truth is we all have messed up, so face that fear—whatever it is. Tell it, "Today, you can out me. You can let the world know I'm a scared grown woman. But guess what! I'm gonna *do it anyway!" I'm gonna soar, be the best mom, and still achieve all my goals. So give me what you got!*

Be an angry woman.

When you stand up to your fears, you'll watch them dissipate. Soon, the "what ifs" have to turn into "why nots." At some point on your journey, whether you believe it or not, you will become stronger. As you sit where you are, can't you see clearly the good life God has for you? I hear you saying, "But I'm stuck." Listen, that's when you should just get mad and say no more! Give yourself permission to take over your life today! Fear no longer resides at your address. Kick it out! Crush it!

I often say, "You outta get mad enough to chase your dreams." Staying stuck doesn't serve you and surely doesn't serve your family. When you begin to move, you build momentum. Momentum will help you crush obstacles sooner. The first time you stand up to your fears will be amazing. I want that for you.

It's time to do the work! Fear has got to go, so are you ready to release it all? Please say yes. I know for a fact that you're ready to move to your next level. You won't know all the answers, but you can do it unafraid. Crush it!

Action Steps:
1. Go over the previous five steps.
2. Journal about what scares you.
3. Write down the worst-case scenarios.
4. Now, write down what could alleviate your pain if the worst case happened.
5. Take each day one day at a time. Enjoy the journey. Watch fear disappear.
6. You get one chance. Rise up! Rock your life!

Journal your thoughts on fear. Why is it imperative that you crush your fears?

_____

_____

_____

_____

_____

_____

_____

_____

STEP 8: GET UP, GET OUT, AND LIVE

A happy mom is a better mom.

Have you ever felt like you were missing something? Like everyone else had found their thing? I know the feeling. But let me tell you that you can get up, out, and live too!

Parenting is a full-time job. We lovingly give all of who we are, and we sometimes look back for that love in return. It comes some days, but it doesn't look the same. And you wonder, "Do they know how much I give?" I know I'm not the only one to feel like this because women tell me this all the time. Let me say it again: Babies cannot show love. They only know how to receive. As we raise them, they begin to be able to reciprocate appreciation and love. So hear what I'm saying: You can bend over backwards and give all you have, but your babies are not designed to give 100 percent back. They're looking to you to provide.

"Wow!" you say. "Why so deep?" Well, I want you to stop looking for your meaning and absolute fulfillment in your kids. You were made for relationship. We all are. That means you've got to get up and get out of your house in order to live.

The entire point of this book is to get you living, loving, and thriving in your zone of greatness. I say that many ways, but you get the gist. *It's time for you to live!*

Living inside your purpose will change your life.

Single parenting is not the end. You're only getting started. Yes, you're a single mom, but you're also a person who loves to live. Trust me, you can still do both!

We all have a zone of greatness. We all have a purpose to chase and achieve. We all have a right to enjoy our lives. So often, the people who kept us from living are long gone, but we still punish ourselves by just existing. That parent who left isn't in the house subsisting. They're out living! And, sis, it's time for you to do the same.

After being stuck and unable to date or go out with friends for years, the very first thing I couldn't wait to do was get up, out, and live. Yes, ma'am! I was bursting with excitement to be … *me again.*

See, I spent years focusing on the babies. I'm glad I did, but it's bad when you feel like you have to choose between happiness and parenting. The truth is I didn't know then what I know now. And what I know is that help was there in the form of other people the whole time. I just had to learn to build my tribe instead of looking for friends and family to fill in for me.

If I could give you any advice to help you in the dating arena, it would be to stop hiding behind being busy and the fact that you're a single mom. So what?! Everyone is busy and everyone has stuff. You and your amazing self need to begin living again. Let's talk about how.

Why Now is a Good Time to Live

It's important for you to have your "me" time with girlfriends and eventually a love interest of your own. Why? Honey, you gotta live more because a happy mom runs a happy home. Your kids can tell when you're unhappy. Trust me. I don't care if you try your darnedest not to show it. They can *see* it.

Give yourself the things you know you need so that you can be all-in when it comes to parenting.

I can hear a scripture so clearly from the Bible: "God sets the lonely in families." If God says you need people, you need people.

Get out of your uncomfortable zone and make what is uncomfortable your conquest!

Now is the best time for you to live. Listen, what child wants to say, "My mom devoted herself to us, and we're thankful, but she's so weird now. We have to keep her company because she doesn't have anybody but us." Sorry. I know that stung, but I want you to know that you having a life and enjoying it is not hurting your kids. It's helping them see how adults are supposed to interact with each other. They're learning that even when you face adversity, you gotta have a love for life that your trials cannot take.

Will you get up? Will you get out? Will you choose to chase all your dreams you've tucked down inside? Let me tell you another story:

My first date as a single mom who hadn't dated in three years was awful. My kids' barber recommended the guy. He was a gigantic dude (and I like 'em

81

tall), no fun, completely unable to relax, and frankly he scared me—not in a "he'll harm me" kind of way but in a "I'm way too big to be talking to this little lady" kind of way. He must have been eight feet tall. We muddled through lunch and talked once or twice after, but I wasn't feeling Sasquatch and he wasn't feeling library lady. But you know what? I went on a first date. I did it! What's the point? Well, hopefully you laughed and you got the point that the first time may not be magic, but get up and live!

The How

How do you get up, out, and live? Well, I alluded to it—you gotta get uncomfortable. Let me tell you a secret: I'm an introvert. If I had my way, I'd be in solitude and working on dreams all day. I can blissfully hang out with myself. Really! But my purpose and my passion require me to be an extrovert, so I've learned to get outside my comfort zone and live. I'm proud to say that I love people. I'm also able to enjoy being with myself for hours on end, which scares some folks. If being alone with yourself makes you uneasy, I'd like to challenge you to do that more. Remember, this chapter is about you being able to move in your awesome by connecting with others. But who are these people meeting if you don't know yourself? Think about it. Getting comfortable with others won't do you any good unless you are first comfortable with yourself.

"How to do more living" is found simply in your ability to get uncomfortable quickly. You'll find that the more you move into areas that scare you, the sooner you'll conquer them and feel more comfortable about your new life. I want you to soar in this area, so below I list three ways to get on your way to living your new and improved life:

1. *Make it a point to meet new people.*
   I keep coming back to people because you cannot make it alone. We can somewhat thrive alone, but we need others if we really want to soar. Life is just easier with people to go all the way with us. That's why chapter 3 is so important. You must find your tribe.

   Meeting new people can mean in business, it can mean platonic relationships, or it can mean love interests. We all have something to offer each other.

   But our treasures go undiscovered if we're too shy to show who we really are.

2. *Be intentional about going new places.*
    Hanging around the same ole places will give you the same ole things. Get adventurous and try new things, food, hobbies, and places. Do the things you've dreamed of doing—don't go overboard, but try something new. It will bless you and give you a new perspective. Who knows whom you will meet and what you'll discover.

    I had traveled only to Jamaica before becoming a Spanish student. When I went to Costa Rica the first time, my entire mindset shifted. I knew on that first trip that I would one day have a second home there. Now I wouldn't hold that dream or love going there had I not tried it. What are you missing out on because you're too comfortable where you are? Hmm? Get up! Get uncomfortable.

3. *Volunteer to do something bold and outside the box.*
    Living our best lives is, for the most part, all about us, but we can also impact others on our journey. Volunteering can expose you to a new, wonderful world as well. You can volunteer to help people in various ways. This can be a civic duty, a project at work, in your community, or something you create yourself. What new life are you missing out on by not connecting with others in an act of service?

These are just a few things that you can do to get up, out, and on to living your best life. Add your own ideas here, but just be sure to move. Your action is the missing piece to your prosperity. Honey, you have to go after it!

It's not the failing that makes me cringe. It's the failing and not trying again that I can't stand.

What? You thought this section wasn't going to include work? Oh honey, living your best life takes courage and action. You've got to do something to have it.

And to have your best life, you've got to want it so bad you do the uncomfortable.

But I guarantee that if you'll try me in this, you'll see that it wasn't as bad as you thought *and* it's actually fun. Yep, you're going to love it!

Now, when is a good time to start living when you have kids at home? My answer: Right now. You've made it this far, so that means you trust me.

Thank you. I appreciate your trust, so I want you to know I was the scared single mom who wanted to get out and live but didn't know how. I was there, but I knew I couldn't stay there. I knew that I had to move past that point, and one way I did that was to face the icky feeling of being uncomfortable and the possible fears my mind was sending my way. You'll have those moments, too. But my question to you again is "Is it worth it to be alone? Or do you want your best life?"

Your best life is absolutely a possibility. The work to get there is up to you.

Action Steps:
1. Get uncomfortable.
2. Journal about the fears you still have. Think of situations that make you uncomfortable.
3. Figure out a way to approach one of your fears head-on.
4. Celebrate your growth.
5. Repeat steps 1-4.
6. Meet new people.
7. Start something new that you're passionate about.
8. Try something new that you've been curious about.
9. Introduce your kids, family, and friends to your new hobby, interest, and/or passion.
10. Rock your life!

Journal your thoughts:

_____

_____

_____

_____

_____

_____

_____

_____

_____

_____

STEP 9: CHASE YOUR DREAMS WHILE WAITING FOR BOAZ

PART I

Setting up a case for love

I love to tell the story of Ruth and Boaz because it gives hope to every divorced mom, single sister, or single mom like me that good girls win. Ever heard of this short story? It's a great story of blessing and deliverance out of hard times for two women who decide to stick together. It goes like this:

Ruth was married, but her husband died. In fact, her husband's dad and brother died too, leaving three women widowed and without the means to survive. So after all their losses, Ruth's mother-in-law, Naomi, decided she would go back to her homeland of Judah because she had heard that God had blessed the people with good crops. Ruth decided to go back with Naomi while the other daughter-in-law, Orpah, returned to her people.

Now in this story, they were sad and widowed. Based on social status and the way women were treated then, they needed to marry. Naomi wanted to know why Ruth would hang on to her at a time like that. She said, "Even in my old age, if I were to marry today, would you wait on me to raise up a son for you to marry?"

Ruth said, "I'm going wherever you go." Pause right there and think about the people you have in your life that will go "all the way" with you. That's a gift. Notice Orpah went back to her people. There's a lesson here: Some people are meant to go all the way with you, some are meant to be there temporarily and so they're in your life for a season. The same happens when we date. Every man you meet is not your Boaz. Keep that in mind, and you'll save yourself a lot of heartache.

Back to Ruth and Boaz's story: Once they were settled in Naomi's homeland, Ruth asked if she could go into the fields and pick up stalks of grain left by the workers. Naomi said yes, so Ruth began to do this in the field of a man named Boaz. I like to tell women all the time that it was right here that Boaz found his Ruth. Ruth was working. She was not in Red bottoms and lounging; she was working and chasing her purpose—a word on what each of us should always be caught doing.

Make no mistake about it, Boaz picked her because he noticed her work ethic, her loyalty to her mother-in-law, her virtuousness, and her laser focus on her purpose. So what should you be doing while you wait on your Boaz? The same thing! Get laser focused on what you want, but let your virtue shine through.

Like Ruth, you should be out making your dreams happen.

Her dream began as simple service to her mother-in-law. My sister, service is key to opening doors in your life. If you want a husband, you need to know that service is a huge part of marriage. Ruth served her mother-in-law selflessly. She wasn't looking for a man. Read the passage. Naomi showed her how to clean herself up and gracefully pick up the wheat Boaz was allowing her to grab. She wasn't chasing Boaz, but she was allowing herself to be found. Then Naomi got the "intel" and had her do all the right things to let him know she was marriage material. But make no mistake; Boaz had already noticed her. He didn't make a move, but he noticed her. Who knows who is watching you or me right now? What I'm getting at is you want a good man, right? Then carry yourself as if he's watching. He could be on the perimeter of your life, checking to see if you're loyal, serving, and demonstrating the quality he thinks you possess. So, sis, let your light shine.

As you parent alone, don't get so focused on dating and marrying just anybody. Prepare for a good man that deserves you. How can you know what you deserve? Well, you must get your vision right. *What you see for yourself is what you will attract.* Ruth wasn't looking for Boaz, but she also wasn't looking for just anybody either. She wasn't behaving like a desperate woman. We know many in the same situation would have tried to remarry. Not Ruth. She was all about serving her mother-in-law. She and her mother-in-law used their heads and worked to pick up what they could to survive. By and by, *as she was living*, she caught the attention of a man who could use what she possessed. She was showing that she was more valuable than just a pretty face. She was *the* woman to have by his side.

So what can we learn from Ruth? There are so many nuggets in this little four-chapter book. I recommend you read it for yourself. But I noticed ten things that will bless you as you continue to live out your awesome and patiently wait for the love you deserve.

1. *Work your purpose.*
    When her husband passed, her purpose became caring for and going wherever her mother-in-law went. As life moved on, her purpose

became to be the wife of Boaz and the great-grandmother of King David. Her willingness to move forward in her life put her in the lineage of God. I'm a Christian, so you know this story gets me geeked up. Who knows what you'll encounter as you keep moving forward. An amazing life is ahead of you when you work your purpose!

2. *Serve others (your babies first).*
She served her aging mother-in-law who, like her, had lost it all. She kept on serving. There are no signs that she murmured, complained, or helped begrudgingly. As you live expecting love to come to you, be found serving. Our babies come first, so that's a given that we take care of home first. Your Boaz will be proud of your ability to parent so well when he meets you.

3. *Prepare for what you want.*
THIS! This is key. You want to be married. You want to have the love of your life. This you must prepare for. When Boaz was allowing Ruth to pick what she needed in the field, neither of them was thinking marriage. She was thinking survival. He was thinking, "Let me help." Naomi preps Ruth for marriage and tells her what to do and where to go. Who is the modern-day Naomi in your life that you need to listen to? I don't know about you, but I pay really close attention to people with relationships I admire. Those great ones make me hold out for my greater.

Listen, as you prepare for your Boaz, you gotta be willing to let the ones who don't measure up—and you know what I mean—go.

4. *Be patient.*
Good things take time. Be patient. Don't go make a Boaz out of the cute guy you meet. Ruth was patient. She wasn't rushing to get married. Read the little book. She went through some seasons before her time came. So it is with you. *Enjoy your season of singleness.* Live! Serve! Love! Travel! Do! Be patient. Your good man is coming. Keep your eyes open.

5. *Be loving.*
I always say confidence is sexy—because it is. Men will tell you that too. But they also want a loving woman. Not bitter. Not angry. Not

overworked and stressed out. Loving. After all, Ruth lovingly uncovered Boaz's feet and lay there as a sign that told him, "If you let me, I will love and serve you." Honey, that's all Boaz needed. He was sold!

I'm not saying love everybody or give your love to everyone who comes by. But we can be loving by seeing about people, checking on them, and giving them a good smile and a nice word.

Don't let your Boaz encounter you not looking like his Ruth.

6. *Be creative.*
Honey, Ruth was like, "Look, I'm gonna pick up some of that barley these folks are leaving behind." Struggling was not something she wanted to do. She got creative and ... humble. It took humility to be a servant when who knows what she had when her husband was alive. But she found herself in a season of lack. We single moms know what lack is. Whether we have all the financial means in the world, something is missing. You and I have to learn to be creative in a season of lack. Ruth humbled herself and worked in the field to survive.

As you rock your life by showing up where you are called, get creative about what that looks like to you. It was her ability to see an opportunity and capitalize on it that got her in front of her Boaz. I didn't say connive for a man. I said be creative. Smile.

7. *Be wise.*
Every man isn't your Boaz. Plain and simple. We know that. Some folks look like him and we sure want them to be, but life won't let it be so. In that day, be wise and let them go. Be wise like Ruth. Note, we see no mention that she was going from man to man asking them to marry her. She wasn't with Boaz seven years, waiting on him to pick her. She was wisely serving her mother-in-law and so singularly focused on that that she was full and happy.

In your preparation and selection, be wise. I want you happy, healthy, whole, healed, and in love, but not with a fake Boaz that's just "for the moment." Honey, you deserve your *lifetime Boaz*, a man to love you for life. Be wise and watch out for the qualities you know you want in a man. Stick to your standards and let them call you picky. It's called being wise and levelheaded.

8. *Be a lady.*
    We all became single moms due to various circumstances. People can have their ideas. I don't care about that. What I do care about is what you think about yourself and what your kids think. Be a lady at all times. Let Boaz and his cousins wait for the love you have to give. One thing I've learned in my life: men may not wait for you, but they sure will respect the fact that you made them wait.

    As you date and meet people, remember your kids are watching. Let's show them how to live life and crush it without a mate. Let them see that when the mate comes, you don't lose your head. You are just as calm, collected, and demanding of respect.

    A little hunger is just what a man needs to realize he needs what really satisfies. A good woman made just for him is what Boaz needs. Be that lady for him. Make him wait.

9. *Be expectant.*
    Like I said, single doesn't mean desperate. Enjoy your life NOW, but expect your love to come. I love when I'm in the throes of something because I always meet people unexpectedly. That singular focus on my purpose is attractive. Now, I don't stop for everybody, and I encourage you to do the same. However, you need to know he may come at the most inopportune time. Be expectant. Be prepared.

    There is no indication Ruth was desperate. She was almost destitute, but still she wasn't desperate. I know she went back with Naomi because the God of Naomi was a Provider. Naomi still had her faith after being in a different land. When that season ended, she went home. She knew there was blessing at home. Surely it was. So you need to know that being single doesn't mean losing your head. Be expectant, honey. There's blessing waiting on you like it was for these ladies.

    There's a man looking for what you bring to the table!

    "Expectation" is a strange word, but you should learn to embrace it. I don't mean checking every second to see if it has materialized, but make it a practice to expect good to come into your life; it'll change your mindset and outlook. Do you know that change can be good? Go on! Try it!

Expect a good day, a good man, and a good life! Be expectant!

10.   *Watch God bless you as you honor him and your family.*
      Because Naomi heeded the call to return home, Ruth got a husband out of the deal. God honored two ladies who had loved and lost by restoring them and placing them in history as two women of faith to mimic.

      As you provide for your babies and do your utmost, God sees that. He knows you need a helpmate. He will provide. I believe it. Just watch.

Ruth teaches us so much, but the lesson that sticks out in my mind is Ruth was going after *her preservation*. She had a mother-in-law too weak to work, and culturally at that time, women could only do so much. Marriage wasn't on Ruth's mind. Notice that. What was on her mind was living. That's what I want you to do. I want you to live, but not just live—survive.

When your back is against the wall, your greatness shows up. There is nothing like being down but knowing you aren't out. *When you have a Ruth and Naomi moment and you keep going, that, my sister, is a sign of the greatness within.* Guess what? You're greater than where you were, where you are, and what you're going through.

I want you to know you have it within yourself to overcome. If you ever had a broken heart, you know what it's like to lose. But when you got over it, you knew what it was like to love. These two women had loved and lost. They were journeying back home for some sign of greater. What they didn't know was that God was using their story to change the world. Ruth's story is not just a love story. It's a story that started the lineage of God himself on Earth. Anybody else glad Ruth found Boaz that day?

What you're going through now will one day bless someone else.

As you go about living your life and walking in your purpose, you'll find that you'll attract better men. Do you know what will bring them to you? Your light, your peace—the real you will bring the right man your way. Be confident always. Be fearless in showing your awesome qualities. Be determined to wait on a good love that's more than worthy of you.

There are no more days of dating people "just because." The days of dating because he has status, money, clout, or is a good person are over. You're now dating on your level. I know you can see yourself in Ruth. Ruth isn't the only one who can find love after tragedy and heartache. So can you! But Ruth made a decision. She decided she wouldn't stay stuck. She got up and journeyed with her mother-in-law to a land she didn't know. She kept working by her side and moving in the direction of something better until one day she caught the attention of a man deserving of her love.

Bring the real you to the forefront and watch your life change.

PART II

How to Date as a Single Mom

Dating can be tough in and of itself. Add in a few kids, and it looks like guys don't want to date you! Have you see these guys lately? I have, and you know what? I say "thank you" in advance. I don't want a man that can't get to know me because I have kids. That tells me his maturity level is too low for me. If you meet a guy like that, tell him no explanation needed and thank you. He just helped you dodge a bullet. Now, people have the right to not have kids if they don't want them. But they don't have the right to make you feel undateable because you do. Dismissed! Okay!

So, how do you date as a single mom? Here is some of my best advice from living it myself.

First, let's revisit the story of Ruth and Boaz. I want to break down Boaz for you so that you can seek qualities in your prospects similar to his. Listen, if God thought enough to show us how not to go after a man, then we ought to listen. Boaz went after Ruth once what he saw lined up with what he already knew he wanted. Yes, a man doesn't just decide to marry. Boaz was looking to marry, but he hadn't found his Ruth. Don't think you will never marry!

Your Boaz is coming as you prepare to be his Ruth.

Qualities a good man has in common with Boaz:

1. *He is kind.*
   Boaz allowed Ruth to gather barley in his field multiple times and for as long as she needed. He saw their needs and showed kindness. There is no indication that he wanted anything more as the story begins.

2. *He is patient.*
   When Naomi saw that Ruth could be saved (basically, they were in need of a miracle as women at that time were taken care of by their husbands), she instructed Ruth on what to do. She goes down to Boaz's threshing floor and lies beside him. Chile, Boaz wakes up and note—he doesn't have a long night of passion. No. He says, "Girl, get up before folks see us and let me go do this thing right." I paraphrased, but he was patient enough to wait for what he wanted.

If you're abstaining or are celibate, don't take any wooden nickels; your Boaz will wait for you.

3. *He is trustworthy.*
    He went and talked to the kinsmen redeemer who was next in line to marry Ruth. He kept his word. He did what was needed to have her hand in marriage the right way.

    We all know what fine looks like. But a fine brother who lies is the worst kind of man to have. How can you sleep at night? Girl, pass on the ones who cannot hold your trust. They just aren't ready. Listen, life's too short to be with someone who doesn't see the gift in having you by his side. *Too short.*

4. *He is respectful.*
    Again, Boaz didn't fuss at Ruth when he saw her "illegally" in his fields. Ruth had asked Naomi if it was okay to go behind the workers because she didn't want to offend Naomi. There's no indication she ever asked the owner of the field. In fact, Boaz said to let her grab what she needed and to put some of the good stuff down for her too.

    He didn't embarrass her or disrespect her because of the state she was in. He showed the utmost respect. We can learn so much here. A man who puts you down doesn't help you and always has an excuse as to why he cannot show you support or respect. Let him go.

5. *He will cover you.*
    Naomi instructed Ruth to go down to the threshing floor and wait until he was cheerful and in a good mood. Ruth did. She uncovered his feet and lay there. I can see Boaz now: He's startled to have a beautiful woman there, especially one that isn't his wife. So he quickly asks, "Who are you?" Ruth reminds him, and he says, "Because you didn't go after a younger man, now you won't have to worry about a thing."

    Notice, he still didn't lose his head because she chose him. She lay there at his feet all night long. In the morning, he went through the proper channels to redeem her. Listen, a good man will cover you. Naomi and Ruth were saved by a man who was kind, patient, trustworthy, and respectful and who had the capacity to cover them. That, my sister, is a word.

In this chapter, you learned that love *can* be yours. Now, I'm not promising the next guy is it or that he has to be perfect. I'm only saying that real love is out there, and to have it, you have to be *whole*. *When you're healed, you see better meaning and you make better decisions about the relationships in your life.* Do the work necessary to have the love and the life you say you want.

We all want a Boaz. But are we a Ruth?

Action Steps

1. Assess the way you date. Who do you normally go for? Do you need to adjust this?
2. Make a list of the qualities you liked in the guys you've dated.
3. What didn't you like and why?
4. What worked in your best relationship? What didn't?
5. Be open to love. Be selective. "Open" doesn't mean take anything that comes by. It means have a heart that's capable of receiving love, but a mind that watches the fruit of every man that approaches you.
6. Broaden your horizons. Try dating new types of people with various backgrounds and interests. You learn and grow more when you do this. Black women are especially loyal in this area but black men are not because they have realized that a good woman may not look like them. Date good men ladies. Don't just make sure he's from the same ethnic group as you. You could be missing out on your good love.
7. Always try again. Love is out there. Be willing to seek it.

Remember, reflecting on our choices helps us see our progress as we move toward our best lives

Journal your thoughts on love and your readiness for it.

_____

_____

_____

_____

Do the work. Your Boaz deserves a Ruth!

STEP 10: SET BOUNDARIES

Protect Your Space. Everybody Isn't Glad You're Healed.

Now that you've moved into your healed and happy place, it's time to protect it so that you can stay that way. Becoming a single parent was never the plan, right? Chile, don't I know it! But you've made it, and you'll continue to do so. Give yourself props for that. You made it through something most people couldn't, and now you know why some walk away. Honey, you rock! But rocking in the midst of adversity doesn't make everyone excited for you. I'm sure you've encountered the ones for whom boundaries were made: the ex, the jealous family member, the boss that doesn't understand—even the bestie who sometimes has a sly remark. Oh yes, as long as you are down and struggling, some folks are glad about it.

In this chapter, I want to discuss protecting your peace and space by setting boundaries.

As you move into your purpose and get comfortable rocking your life (as God intended), you'll find that people will have various ideas about you, but I'm here to tell you to move on anyway. When you begin to notice commentary or behavior you don't like, make a note of it and set boundaries. Boundaries tell people how to treat you. If you don't speak up, some folks will take too much liberty. So protect your space ... and protect your heart.

Why Boundaries Are Healthy

Think of it like this. You own a home. Your home has a fence around it, and so does your neighbor's. Why? Because you want to protect your property, and they want to protect theirs. Now that you're healed and ready to love again, *old loves can't come back*. Why give them a second chance when they couldn't handle the first? Listen, it's up to you, but if you decide to let old or new loves in, have your boundaries set long before the first date.

Setting Boundaries at Home

Your kids need to know you have boundaries they cannot cross. This plays into respect and how they view you. Every child needs to know their parent has a look, a tone, and a *particular* side that means, "Aw shucks! We're in trouble now." A good healthy dose of boundaries is just what your kids (and mine) need. Likewise, you need to have boundaries as you deal with your kids. Fussing and screaming, etc. simply won't do, and they won't respect you. Hey, I've been there. You know what moves them? *Consequences*. I have a discipline checklist under my Parent Resources tab, and you can check it out anytime at KaywandaLamb.com. I made it with you in mind.

When we have an understanding between our kids and us, when they know what is expected of them our home lives are better. Not perfect, but better. Set boundaries. You'll be glad you did.

Setting Boundaries at Work

I think it's important to mention this here even though I could write an entire book on decorum. Work is work. We should make sure we're showing up in excellence every day. As ladies, we shouldn't be the diffuser of gossip or the purveyor of mess on our jobs. If you're a victim of such behavior, set boundaries immediately. People treat you the way you allow them to treat you. A good healthy dose of HR (human resources) always helps to get people in line. But at the onset of such behavior, stand up for yourself.

I bring this up because I have experienced hurt at work. I know the pain of having to provide for my children and work under duress. After you've done all you can—you've contacted HR, etc.—please know that we're not meant to be in mess, and sometimes things like this happen to move us closer to our destiny. Sometimes it's a pain point in our lives because God is nudging us elsewhere, and if HE didn't allow it, we'd be comfortable somewhere He no longer is. Prayerfully consider what's right for you, set a plan of escape (it may not be immediate), and execute it by looking for a blessed place that will appreciate your talents, resources, and abilities. It's out there!

Setting Boundaries in Love

This section will be long because I want you to really get how the failure to set boundaries continues to bring the same type of guy back into your life. I mean … haven't you noticed that you can break up with a guy, spend time alone, heal, and the very next guy looks different but is the same? How does that happen? You must watch the signs and pay attention to warnings that this type of guy is giving you. Yes, it takes work to do this. No, I don't like it either, but your peace, time, and heart are worth the extra diligence.

Setting boundaries starts by first understanding why you need them and *deserve* them in the *first place*! Read on.

It's the little things.

Let's say you've gone through your healing process and you're ready to date again. You meet a fine, fantastic, smart, funny new guy, and he's your dream. (Cue the choir.) Except ... maybe he does little things that annoy you. I mean itsy-bitsy things that ... you know, you can overlook.

He may do things like call you late at night when you previously advised him you have to be asleep by 10:00 p.m. He may ask you about sex when you already told him you're celibate. He may do little things that annoy you but aren't red flags to other folks. I'm here to tell you that they're signs that he has some growing up to do, or he may have some deeper issues.

Let's face it! No one is perfect. Little things about people you date are going to irk you. That's not what I mean here. I mean you can look over time and see a pattern where he's always second-guessing you, making you rethink your decisions, nit picking, and doing tiny things that over time become big things. Look out. I like to call this one the "I don't know how to love, so I annoy" guy. He's immature and manipulative. He doesn't deserve your time, and you cannot heal him. He has to accept he has a problem and work to fix it.

What boundary can you set? Well, you let him know exactly what you see and are feeling. Now, to be clear, you should give him a chance (if you like him) to correct his actions and allow him time to show you he can put those behaviors behind him. If he cannot, you know what to do ... bye Felicia!

Maybe it's the big things.

Set boundaries because it only takes one big no-no from a love interest for you to think back on all the warning signs you saw. Listen, talking about you, calling you names, causing scenes—or worse—putting his hands on you. Chile, that would be the last time, right? So how do you make sure you set boundaries when you're dating? Read on:

1. *Know your worth.*
    People say this a lot. Let's break it down. Knowing your worth really means "loving you" so much that anything outside the way you treat

yourself HAS to go! You've got to know how you want to be treated going into a relationship. If you see deal-breakers, speak up, advise him how he should treat you, and have a consequence waiting when he doesn't follow your lead.

2.   *Know your deal-breakers.*
The wrong time to know what your "No he didn't" moments are is in the throes of a fight, verbal or physical. Please take some time to jot down what you absolutely are not "here for."

Example: Lying, stealing, cheating, emotional abuse (he got you up and down emotionally and he likes it), physical abuse (no explanation needed) … I could go on, but I'm gonna stop here and say: No man is worth your time, your energy, or your life. If you find yourself in any of these—leave.

Most of us are single moms, so if kids are involved, *you need to understand that staying in any foolishness is teaching your kids that it's okay.* Break free. Don't allow anyone to make you feel less than or treat you like it. Honey, you're a Queen! He must bow down or at best worship the ground you walk on—that's the mindset I want you to have because it's true. You are worthy of good love.

3.   *Know your plan of attack.*
As you embark on dating, have your game plan ready. Life has taught me to be prepared instead of reacting to what happens. Dating is one of those things we can't just do without a plan. It seems easy, but it isn't when we fall for someone and they begin to mistreat our heart, trust, and love. Know in advance what you'll use to stand up for you.

Examples:
1.   You can have a heart-to-heart if you think they may not notice the behavior that's bothering you.
2.   Take a breather and give yourselves some space.
3.   Release them back into the sea of men and pick another one.
4.   Contact authorities if they're more than annoyed by your breakup.
5.   Don't live in fear of what they'll do, causing you to do nothing.
6.   Love yourself first.

I know this seems like a weird lesson, but so many women struggle in relationships because they won't exercise their right and strength to demand people treat them with respect. I was once that woman. I had the wishy-washy feelings, the back-and-forth of "does he love me" when he was clearly showing me he didn't. I want you happy, healthy, whole, and healed. So, from experience I can tell you that real love is clear. Real respect is clear. There's no guesswork involved when people care about you. There's no mistreating you and calling it love. Break away from anyone who harms you and calls it love.

To some this may seem obvious. For others, it's just what you needed. Honey, we all are on a journey. We all have a process. Allow yourself to grow. If this was you and you have learned, awesome! If this is you, step back and look to see if where you are is where you want to be. Then do something about it.

You deserve good love. Real love. True love. Demand it. Protect it. Wait for it.

Action Steps:
1. Get to know yourself before you get to know anyone else.
2. Create a list of deal-breakers that show you which relationships you need to evaluate and/or release.
3. Surround yourself with people who are for you so that you can withstand the temptation to return to unhealthy love.
4. Continue to reflect on your relationships and make changes accordingly.
5. You don't owe anyone anything. You owe yourself everything. Love yourself enough to walk away from not good enough relationships that keep you stuck. You'll be glad you did!

Journal your thoughts on boundaries. Have you had to set boundaries in the past? What are your deal-breakers?

_____

_____

_____

_____

_____

Have a plan. Set boundaries. They protect you.

STEP 11: REMEMBER THE STRUGGLE

It's okay to look back. Just don't go back.

When I think about the drama I went through as a young single mom, it pales in comparison to the joy I have now as a strong single mom who's chasing EVERY dream and taking ZERO prisoners.

It may be hard for you to imagine me being thankful for the pain, but I am. Now, I don't want to go through it again. Oh no! But I see how my survival and ultimately my ability to thrive in the face of turmoil has allowed me to help other women come up and out of their dark places. It is with this in mind that I want you to never forget the struggle. Don't glory in it. No! But never forget. Share your story to help others and always be mindful to step in when another mama needs help. Always.

Growing up in the South, my grandmother talked a lot about purpose and that each of us has a job to do in life. I saw the struggle. We were poor, but they always made sure we had food to eat. I look on those years growing up not with disdain, but with joy. Yes, we struggled some, but what I remember mostly is the love we shared as a family.

If I can look back on struggle and smile, I must be crazy, right? Nope. I'm every bit of sane, but going through something and coming out okay makes you appreciate it all the more. So why am I asking you to remember the struggle of your single-parenting days? I can hear you now: "I'm in this, Kaydy, with no end in sight."

Listen, one day, you won't have a broken heart. One day, you'll marry and love again. One day, you'll be happy, whole, healthy, and healed. One day, these times of single parenting will be a memory. Yes, sister, it won't always be like this.

You'll rise from this place of single parenting and doing it alone. Trust me. It's the law of life.

Newton says, "An object in motion remains in motion." I want you to keep moving and looking for your brighter days. I want you to enjoy the days you have right now. But I want you (when all of this is a blur and you're healed) to remember to help another sister going through the same.

See, we go through struggles to help other people. Don't think this was designed to tear you down and keep you from rising again. Yes, raising children with a broken heart is hard. It'll heal. Yes, raising children after divorce, when the other parent walks away, is hard. You'll make it. Yes, it's gut wrenching to have to parent alone because the awesome love of your life died unexpectedly and you're left to live a life you never planned for. I know, but you're gonna make it. And when you do, help another sister see how she can too.

The only reason I can talk to you and tell you how to handle moving on is that I've done it myself. I sit here in peace and with total forgiveness because I did the work to heal and MOVE ON. It wasn't easy. I won't lie to you, but I knew deep inside me that it was necessary. What are you learning on your journey that's necessary so that you can grow to your best self? You should remember the struggle, yes, but put it away. Be thankful for it all, but put it away.

I want you to start writing down your journey. I want you to be able to one day look back at all you have overcome. I want you to smile, knowing you did your best and you made it! Oh yes, girl, you're gonna make it!

Sometimes you gotta go through to grow.

I use the above phrase on Twitter often. I post a great deal of motivation for the single mom, and I find that it's in our tough times that we grow more than we ever would if life was nice. Oh, I know! I was like, Lord, why can't it be better? Why is it hard? But you know what? Those tough times grew me up. I'm stronger because life whipped me. Can you hear me laughing? I'm laughing and simultaneously thinking, "I can't believe I'm thankful for the rough times, but I am." One day, you will be too!

Sis, you can shy away from moving in your destiny, or you can look at your life right now and decide that you and your babies will thrive. You can decide to do all the work I've asked you to do in this book, and then you can move into your blessed place. Oh yes, you can! So how do you remember the struggle and not let the pain paralyze you? Read on.

How to Truly Thrive

Every great person you know had a valley moment where they were down but not out. They had to find it in themselves to soar again. They had to learn to thrive. Like you and me, their situation looked bleak. But you know

what made the difference? Their joy, their vision, their knowing were all based on what they could see and almost touch. You've got to decide that no matter what has come against you, you're going to make it.

You simply decide within yourself that you'll make it. Another tip is to utilize all the teachings that have served you up to this point in your life. Combine what you knew with what you know and move in the direction of destiny.

So, as you can see, it's a simple decision to be your best self. Combine all the qualities you like about yourself or that you see in others and you want to emulate, and let's make your progress happen. No one can stop your movement but you.

Recalling is a part of healing.

As you've moved from vulnerable to being alive again, you've discovered that many people have been hurt, but they didn't stop there. They didn't let the hurt stop them from getting to their "better" or their "greater." You, too, have to dig down deep and decide that's what you're going to do. In all your moving and growing, I want you to remember what you went through. I just don't want you to settle on it.

When you can remember what you went through and not curse your singleness, you're healed. When you can tell the details to a friend of yours and not cry or fuss, you're healed. When you can remember your struggle (s) and not hate anyone involved, but say "Thank You Lord" for it all, you're healed. Keep moving toward that place. It's coming!

Action Steps:
1. Always remember what you went through.
2. Don't let it define you.
3. Let it fuel you to be better, date better, want better, know better.
4. Spend the time you need to make peace with parenting alone.
5. Rise! Soar! Be great!

Journal:

STEP 12: DO IT ANYWAY!

You were born great. Everything you've gone through came to stop you.
It lost.

I am so strong-willed when it comes to achieving my dreams. That's one quality no one had to teach me. I know what I want and I go after it. Now, I may have sat on the bench longer than I should have, but when I got in the game—look out!

I'm so fired up about the women reading this book right now! I'm fired up about YOU because I know you're primed to go make your dreams happen, to take your family to the next level, and to change the course of history. Yes, I really believe this book is that strong. The proof comes in whether or not YOU make a move. See, I'm chasing my dreams. You reading my book right now is a dream come true. I'm elated that I got to touch you. Now you get to go and touch your kids and other women, and just like that, a ripple is created. Sis, we can change the world if we apply our knowledge, skills, and passion with our purpose.

Where on earth did all my fire and passion come from? Well, my grandmother, Therestha Lamb, was the most resilient woman I've ever met. She made it through life with a third-grade education. She married at fourteen and had twelve kids with a man fifteen years her senior. She *did it anyway!* She worked all her life in lowly jobs, but she gave her all. I know this because she told me. Her desire to be her best at whatever she put her hand to has inspired me to do the same—no matter what it was. That's a great legacy, and I caught it! What will your kids catch from seeing you live? I'm not exempt. I ask myself the same things. *What are my boys learning from how I live, not by what I say?* Hmm … We must make sure to be lights that lead the way and spark ideas and excitement in our kids.

In my early twenties, I caught the desire to be excellent in a relationship that wasn't good for me. I've spent plenty of time, energy, love, and resources in places and with people that didn't deserve my *awesome.* Can you relate?

Listen, we can't beat ourselves up for giving our all to someone or something that didn't understand our beauty. But we can move forward and win! I want to win. Do you want to win in your life? What are you gonna do about it? You know I'm gonna ride this mamma-jammer till the wheels fall off.

We're close to the end of this book, and I want you to know that you and I may have messed up along the way, but our legacy is greatness, healing, wholeness, favor, and a blessed family!

Sis, you've got to *know this* deep down inside you – you deserve to be treated well and to win. When you believe it and allow it to permeate your thinking, *you'll be unstoppable!*

Leaving a Legacy

A more important question is what will your children *catch* from you? We have a saying, here in the South, that what we teach is caught and not taught. Meaning, kids learn by watching what we do and not what we tell them. Think long and hard about what you want them to walk into their destiny carrying. How much of your story will they interpret as their own? I want you to think about that. Keep it in the back of your mind, but let's leave all the negative on the back burner right now. We'll revisit this later.

As you move toward your amazing future, I know you'll push your babies into their destiny with a clean slate, a life of love, and a legacy to fulfill. What you have to figure out is … how.

You've gone through eleven lessons to get you to your blessed place of peace of mind, excitement about your new beginning, and understanding how to run your family and your life with intention. But this last one is all about pulling out the last bit of fire and tenacity within you. This last chapter is about you learning to be courageous without anyone (me, your friends and family, etc.) holding your hand.

This step you do alone. In your going, there is growing. If parents could live for us, they would. Your excellence lies in your ability to chase your portion in life. Do IT!

How to Do It Anyway!

When I use this phrase, there's usually something negative that I don't want to do, but then I rise up and kick booty! Yesss! Sometimes, just choosing to get up and do it all again is a feat. I know it isn't all roses and lollipops every day, and that's why I want to ignite a fire in you. I want you to have a fire that burns so bright that you refuse to let another day of parenting alone make you feel like you're anything less than amazing!

Doing it anyway is all about stepping into the place of a mama lioness—protective, supportive, provider, nurturer. I want you to ferociously go after your goals and your destiny. I want you to parent with all you've got AND chase your dreams. I'm a witness it can be done. How? To do that, you need to have done the work in lessons 1–11. If you skipped around, go back. You and your progress are worth the time it takes to do the work on yourself. This is too important to your progress to miss a step. When you're ready, keep reading.

Doing what you must when you don't feel like it—that, my sister, is the Do It Anyway! spirit. Working your fingers to the bone for the dream you have on the inside and to feed your kids … that's the do it anyway spirit. Disciplining your children when they ought to know better and you've told them a million times … that's the do it anyway spirit. Doing anything when you'd rather be resting or enjoying your life is called tapping into the *do it anyway* inside you. To have what you say you want, you gotta pull those dreams out of you and walk in it. No more wishing. Doing. Chasing.

Your ability to thrive in the face of difficulty not only reminds you that you can do it, but it reminds your kids that you're in control.

Why Your Kids Have to See You Thrive

Like I said that "kids do what they see, not what we say." Well, wouldn't it make sense to you that they have to see you thrive to believe they can make it too? Yes, it does. And you know what? They're going to also learn what it's like to win in the face of adversity by watching you keep your family together, happy, healthy, whole, and healed. Oh yes! Your life is a testimony not just to people outside your family but to your kids as well.

The media loves to throw statistics around like "kids whose moms were single parents will end up single parents too." You know what? I read a post that said girls of single-parent homes went on to become excellent business owners. You can look at the news, but don't believe the hype. So many times we let external factors stress us out. Don't! Keep leading your family the way you were designed to. Your kids will succeed.

Do It Anyway!

It is not what you do for your children, but what you have taught them to do for themselves, that will make them successful human beings. – Ann Landers

I totally agree with this quote. It's one of my faves. Your kids are learning from you. You are showing them that there is no excuse because my mom took care of us. She *did it anyway*! Your pushing through the hard times teaches them that hard times will come, but they can be conquered. Let me just say here that if you don't share the good, the bad, and the not so pretty with them, you should. If they're of age, they should know when times get tough so that they can see how they came out and know how to survive themselves.

Real integrity is doing the right thing knowing that nobody's going to know whether you did it or not. – Oprah Winfrey

I love to talk to my boys about integrity, especially when I hit a bad spot in life or when they have something come up because I get to show them that my faith hasn't wavered and I didn't dare think to do anything unseemly to solve the problem. I stayed levelheaded and kept my faith. Doing that does them more good than me telling them how to behave if that were to happen to them.

The secret to effective single parenting is coming back after you fail, trying again after a not-so-good moment where you lost it, etc. You know, we hate the not-so-good moments, the moments that make us feel inferior when we're truly extraordinary, but we can't change them. Yes, to be a doitanywayer you have to sometimes turn off the guilt cam and say, "Hey, I tried. I'll try again tomorrow too." And let it be. You must develop the ability to shut the guilt cam down and keep moving despite your feelings.

What You and Your Kids Will Gain

Can you imagine the bond between you and your babies after you do the work set out in this book? Can you imagine how much peace you'll have knowing you're on the right track? Can you imagine your better life? I know you can see it, smell it, and touch it. So go get it!

What I'm really asking is, "Are you willing to go create it?" Oh yes, there's no magic fairy dust here. The magic that's about to happen in your life is all you—just a mama that loves her kids and some kids who love their mama working together. You're the leader. Until Boaz comes, you must rise up and lead. No half-leading, laissez-faire parenting—lead! You don't have to know it all to do it all. But you do need to try every moment, every day. You and your kids deserve that.

My boys may not like not having a dad, but they haven't gone without the love and support they need. Not once. When you get close to your kids and get real with them, you'll see your bond flourish. As they begin to notice how "Rock Star" you are, they're going to gain the confidence to do and be the same. So you standing in your smallness is not helping them.

Break out, honey! Be the awesome person you know God made you to be!

Rock the life you got!

I've said this before: "No one picks this life." But we're single parents nonetheless, so what are you going to do about it?

I encourage you to rock the life you got. Show up and show out every day as the awesome mom, leader, career woman, entrepreneur, etc. that you are! Your greatness doesn't stop because some man left or passed away. I know it hurt, but you don't get to stop there. Beautiful little people are depending on you. And you know what? You're gonna show them you can handle this and then some.

So, sweet sister, if you've learned nothing else, I hope you've learned that excuses, hurt, and pain have to go in order for you to rock the life you got! Sis, you're perfectly positioned to do just that!

When you choose to release who hurt you, who walked away, why you feel guilty, etc., you open up your life for blessing. So listen to me: if you want to excel, move in the direction you know life is calling you. Cast your fears aside. I've proven to you that you can do it with kids. Cast your lonely aside. We've talked about how to know Boaz when he comes. There's no more weight holding you down. If you don't move, it's because you don't want to. You now have the pieces to move forward and change your life—forever. Will you? Oh, I know you will!

Action Steps/Combining All the Pieces

This is the part where it all makes sense. Do you know that everything you've gone through came to stop you? But, sis, you made it. It didn't work. You win! But sometimes, we don't see life like this. All that you've gone through is already proof that you are making it and will continue to make it through this season of your life. In this section, we review what we learned and discuss our final actions. Are you ready to rock? I know you are!

I want to challenge you to combine all the pieces of this book with all the pieces of your life. Sure, being born into a wealthy family and marrying Prince Charming would've been better, but this is what you got. And what you got IS beautiful. So let's work what we've got into what we want. That starts with you.

Action Steps: The Final Work

Once you've been honest with yourself throughout this book (maybe even cried a little), I want you to take one last look at the soul work I've asked you to do. All those years ago, I had to do the exact same thing. It was for my good. This is for your good. I know it's hard. *Do It Anyway!*

1. Can you see the value in healing yourself? Why?
2. Do you understand why you must figure out your purpose?
3. Who are the people in your life who support you and your kids?
4. Why must you get clear on the mental, emotional, and physical clutter in your life? How do you eradicate it?
5. What will you organize first?
6. Why is focus so important? Can you commit to one central goal right now? What is it?
7. Why must you be fearless in all situations? What does that do for you? What does it teach your kids?
8. Why must you get up and live? Who benefits from a happy you?
9. How do you date from here on out? What are your deal-breakers?
10. Why are boundaries good?
11. What did the struggle teach you? What if you struggle again? Are you better prepared to rise up and squash it?
12. What promises do you make to yourself to forever stay unstuck and moving forward in purpose, with passion, and on point?

Journal your thoughts:

_____

_____

_____

_____

_____

_____

_____

_____

_____

_____

_____

_____

_____

_____

_____

_____

_____

_____

_____

_____

_____

_____

_____

_____

_____

_____

_____

_____

As you continue on your journey going in the direction of your purpose, please know that I'm rooting for you and so many other moms I may never meet. I know that you have greatness inside you, that you're amazing, and that you're worthy of love.

I want you to know this: Your babies are blessed to have you, and your life will never be the same if you put this information to use. I sat down and poured out what I know helped me go from broken, hurt, stuck, and miserable to loving and living again. I want that for you right now. But my wanting your greater won't cut it. YOU have to do the work. You have to see it for yourself and want it so badly that moving toward it is the next step. Sis, I invite you into the circle of women who Do It Anyway! Come on in, knowing life won't magically get easier, but it will bend to your will if you'll answer the call to rock the life you got!

This book is no magic potion. It's only a guide to help take you from where you are to where you want to go. Learn from a woman who has been where you are and is at peace with it all. No drama, no sorrow, no bitterness—just blessed. Walk toward your healed place of amazing. Walk toward your home full of love, light, and peace. Walk toward your Boaz, knowing you are ready to be his Ruth. Walk toward your blessed life. I believe you can do it. I believe you are ready for it.

I leave you with this:

Your possibilities are endless. You shape your life by the chances you take on your dreams.
Go on, sis!

#doitanyway

BONUS LIFE LESSON:
GET YOUR MONEY RIGHT!

Just cause you broke now don't mean you gotta stay broke always.

I couldn't write a book to help you get your life together as a single mom and not tell you about my shameful yet redemptive financial crises. Yes, hun! Crises. Plural. Remember, this single-parenting journey is just that—a journey. You're going to have highs and lows, no doubt about that, but know that you'll make it through them if you keep pushing!

Crisis 1

When I was pregnant with my first son, I had (for a single chica straight outta college) a decent JOB. I had saved up as much as I could and was prepared. Welp, he was eight and a half pounds and ate up everything! EVERYTHING! And what do good mommas do? We feed our babies and we go with what we know. In retrospect, I could have saved somewhere, but the common sense of a twenty-three-year-old (no offense, young'uns) who thinks she knows it all was not what it is now at thirty-eight. Ha-ha! I was spending money like it was water on the newest gadget, state-of-the-art bottles, and fancy nipples. And did I mention I was getting half the pay? Yep, my bills got behind because I was providing. I later dug myself out of that hole, so my word to you today is if you are in a financial crisis, go through it, know that it gets better, but you and your babies better eat. Make sure you have food, shelter, and clothing. Bill collectors aka Peter and Paul will just have to wait.

So once I got on my feet and was kind of handling life, I got pregnant again. Chile, more problems: broke up with their dad (as you know); daycare was a fool (Kaywanda speak for high as all get out); moved to a bigger, better (more expensive) apartment—and survived. Anybody else thankful for income-tax refunds? Those were my salvation. I learned to pay my rent up three months with my income tax, and that gave me room to breathe and save. What's my point? You've got to quickly learn how to survive as a single mom. Everything that looks pressing … ain't.

Now, what can you learn from my early situation? First, budget and stick to it. Save a little until you can save a lot. Use your income tax and other windfalls you get to pad your savings and pay up your rent (we always need a roof, but a purse and some car rims are not necessities). Use your lump sums wisely. If I could take some of those storms back, I would. But you know what? I learned so much in those seasons of lack that they're the reason I have the wisdom to teach you today.

Oh, my storms didn't stop, although I had some years of blessing. Get ready for the juicy, lavish living and the foolish wasting. Cues orchestra.

Crisis 2

When I moved to Texas, my income increased and so did the cost of living. I was vested in the mortgage company I worked for, so like a nut, I liquidated my stock and 401(k) to help with moving expenses—BAD CHOICE. I then began a debt pay-down process called the Debt Snowball from DaveRamsey.com. My goodness! My savings was growing and so was my personal 401(k). Then, all of a sudden my family needed money, so I lent it. And ... now that I had a little security, I wanted to hang out with this new guy I met/was crushing on/wanted to impress. Honey, between the two, I spent way more than I needed to "kick it." *Don't act like I'm the only one who ever flossed for love!* I know. Ridiculous. So we're going all these places, and I need a new outfit, and guess what? He ain't noticed none of it! I mean really! Oblivious to my good looks and the money I'm wasting trine date his behind. So that didn't break me, but the combination of bad decisions made me low on the totem pole when it came to my budgetary goals.

Add in my son breaking his elbow (which should have never happened) at a football game, and my savings I had worked so hard for dissipated in a matter of months. It had taken me three years to save almost $10,000 on a teacher's salary and just like that ... gone! Ouch! I'm still hurting today. Listen compounding interest is real.

When I said I wanted to talk about finances, one of my cousins said, "But you have debt!" I said, "Just because I have debt doesn't mean I don't have sense!" That's what I have to say to you, sis: Just because you have some debt right now doesn't mean you're going to always have that debt. It's time for you to face it like me and begin to see how you can attack it. Little by little, attack it.

How do you do that? Well, I'm an educator and sometimes I tutor people for extra money. I'm super uppity about my time and my knowledge, so I charge the kind of rate where you have to be serious to book me. Okay! (That means I don't tutor a lot!) But, that is a way to bring in extra funds.

Also, one year, I got a second job for Christmas. It was hell on Earth, but I did it because that's what you do when you want to change your situation— you go through some discomfort to reach your goals. *Capisce?* Can you afford to take a second job sis? Do you have someone you can trust to watch your kids? Can you work for yourself from home and bring in extra funds? Think about these things.

Now, I do have plenty of debt, so I'm no debt guru, but let me tell you this: I read, I research, I study, and I APPLY what I learn. You, sis, have to do the same in order to change your situation. I want you to declare it with me:

I refuse to walk into my destiny with debt. My debt has an expiration date.

Listen, your situation isn't hopeless. It will get better when you get to working on it. I keep saying Boaz wants a Ruth. Get your house in order and be his Ruth. Sis, go into your next relationship light, no burdens, debt-free, and healed. You'll find that will cut out more drama and give you two more time to enjoy life on your terms. You say, "Kaywanda, that's easy for you." No it ain't, but guess what I'm gonna do! Right! Do it anyway! And when you decide to do the same, your situation will change.

I want to list some resources I've used and some I recommend as I'm on this journey with you to conquer my debt. See how keeping it real can heal you and not suffocate you?

Listen, this debt pay down pep talk is not about popularity or bragging. This is about living your best life; it's about getting the best quality of life you can for you and your babies. Don't sit there caring about what folks think.

Work hard until your hard work works for you!

Bankrate.com: This site is reputable and has loads of debt calculators, mortgage calculators, credit card rate comparisons, etc. It's a comprehensive tool to help you see your financial picture. I've looked at it so many times before making decisions. I recommend you begin to compile resources to help you on your journey.

DaveRamsey.com: This guy has impressed me. I want a 0 credit score like him one day with plenty of money in the bank. Okay! Maybe you want an

800? Shoot, a 700, right, sis? (If you have A-1 credit, don't write me. You know I'm generalizing.) But listen, his debt snowball method is my main squeeze. Love it. I'm employing it now by paying the smallest bill off first.

Let me stop right here and say I got overzealous a few times and jumped ahead of myself, trying to pay down a lot of bills at once. Nope. Just do the one and you'll see immediate progress, which then encourages you to keep going. Oh yeah! Been there. Done that. A couple times. This time is for keeps! Woo! Are you in?

Planner/Organizer: I have to know where my money is, where I'm going, what I'm doing, etc., so I have to have a planner. Listen, your life will not resemble what you know it can be unless you get your act together. If you aren't having financial issues, praise the Lord! You can skip this part. But if you know you can use some help, take this section seriously and do the work. Jot down your creditors. Next, jot down the balances. Write down the due dates, minimum payments, and then number them from least to greatest in balance. I had one I HATED so I made it first. HA-HA! Ever got mad at a company? Yep! Paid them off and closed them out.

Get mad at your debt. Get creative about how to pay it off. Get determined and pace yourself. Start small. Start now!

(I love the feel of my planners, so I prefer to have mine in my hand. Digital planners are great too!)

As you can see, I'm passionate about getting debt-free. I have a ways to go, but I'm not giving up, and I'm not letting my disappointment in myself or in life stop me from moving forward. And neither are you! I want you to face it—face it now—so that you can have the life you want.

Planning for Rainy Days

Having gone through some rough patches (I have some other names for them), I get nervous and save as much as I can—as strange as I can. Below I'm going to list some weird ways I save little sums here and there. You can save how you want, but I like to keep money in different places. Listen, life can whip you so bad you'll start hoarding too! Read on.

1. I keep my extra change in a huge pickle jar. When it adds up, I take it to one of those change places at the local grocery (you can take it to

your bank) and voila! I have an extra $60–$200 at the end of the year. Nice, right! Don't despise small beginnings.

2. Another method is to do the $1 a day method. So, $1 for day 1, $2 for day 2, $3 for day 3, and so on. At the end of a year, you'll have more than $365. The power of compounding. Listen, the best thing you can do for yourself in the area of your finances is begin to read up and study how to make your money grow. Again, she's (your money is) climbing up the ladder with you. Start small, sis, but start.

3. Nothing like stuffing a little money in a savings account that requires you to go to great lengths to withdraw the money. I've long since had to liquidate said account, but hey, I'll make another one. This reminds me of Lisa Nichols, a famous motivational speaker, who said she worked a part-time job to get out of her mess and sent all the money to her bank by writing checks weekly. After three years, she goes to check on it and deposit a check. To her surprise she had over $60,000 in the bank. A single mom! Struggling. No idea about compounding interest. But it worked for her! Guess what? It can work for you. Start small with five dollars if you have to. Just start!

4. Lastly, a not-so-crazy way is to invest in a 401(k) or some type of plan your employer has. If they offer matching funds, take it! This allows you to save before or after tax. I like both. Before taxes lets me save on interest and take more money home. After taxes frees me from paying taxes on it later. Check with your financial advisor, and most importantly, get to saving.

Listen, when I left the mortgage company, I had two big checks coming: one for a retirement fund they put up for all employees and my 401(k) I had on my own. Like I said, how foolish of me to liquidate them. At the time, I thought it was best. We live and we learn. So just like I'm moving forward with what I got, you have to do the same.

The Comeback

Are you able to see some of yourself in my money story? I grew up poor. I knew I wanted money and nice things, but I had no idea about investing and truly saving consistently. My grandmother saved but not in a bank, so I thought I knew how to save.

I went to college, got a good job, learned to save. Yay! I did it! But when life got rough, I withdrew it all. Now, what sense did that make? I know. I'm shaking my head. Now I know better, and all I can do is … well, better. Same for you. We *can change* our realities. We *can change* our money stories. We *can change* our lives and our kids' lives. It takes us making the step and getting *focused* on that change we want to see.

I don't know about you, but I'm ready wow myself with how well I can save and get debt free! I want my children TOO blessed to be stressed, and I want grandchildren to be lenders and not borrowers. I'm talking legacy here. What are you leaving your kids? Leave a legacy, sis! Leave them a solid foundation along with the knowledge you've learned on investing and saving.

Now, I just got real naked to show you that I'm so serious about us single moms doing what it takes to have our best lives NOW. What are you going to do to change your situation? Maybe finances aren't a problem for you and you think me foolish to have done what I did? Okay. But where you do struggle, you need to work in that area.

Leave no weakness comfortable in mediocrity. Mold it into the greatness you are designed for!

If you are on Struggle Street like I've been many times, no excuses, boo! Little by little, save what you can. Start now, not later. You can change your situation. My two life crises prove that.

Your blessed life is yours for the taking.

You have one life to make a difference. By chasing your dreams, stepping into who you are, and by getting your money right, you will instill new values in your kids. Show them the greatness that lies within them. Show them how to pull it out. You're now ready to live your best life.

Go get 'em!

No matter how hard it gets, *Do It Anyway!*

Affirmation:

My right now is not my always. I am blessed and highly favored of The Lord. I do not live in lack. I live in abundance. My family has all they need to survive. We not only survive, we thrive. We help others with the overflow of our blessings. Goodness and mercy are ours because we honor God with

our hard work, giving, obedience, and life. What someone else did does not concern me. I accept the call on my life to raise good kids, show them the way to live a blessed life, and together, we *do it anyway!*

You are not fully all you were born to be. Decide today to find out all that life has for you and pursue it with all you've got. You are greater than your situation and your best is yet to come! And when you get tired sis, keep going.

I believe we all have "greatness" within us as Les Brown says. Let the trials of life show you who you really are. You are an overcomer, a strong woman, and an amazing mom! Single is only one word used to describe you among a sea of better ones. Extraordinary, patient, kind, hardworking, beautiful, deserving of love, etc. are words one could use to describe a Rock Star like you. Focus on that and not on what people want you to be or define you as. Then, you will find your strength. Then, you will *do it anyway.*

Many blessings on your journey!

XOXO,

Kaywanda
Your Single Mom Coach

Journal:

1. Where will I begin to attack my finances?

_____

_____

_____

_____

_____

_____

_____

_____

2. Do I need help? Who can I turn to for advice?

_____

_____

_____

_____

_____

_____

_____

_____

3. Why won't I give up now? Who's going to hold me accountable to get my financial house in order?

_____

_____

_____

_____

_____

It won't be easy. It never is, but...Do It Anyway! Change your financial picture and leave a legacy that baffles the next four generations of your family!